PRAISE FOR *GETTING SMART ABOUT RACE*

"In *Getting Smart about Race*, Margaret Andersen provides a lucid and sensitive meditation on racial inequality, analyzing both the origins of American racism as well our current social and political conflicts. Based on rigorous sociological research, this volume is written in an accessible narrative style and will provoke meaningful conversations about our nation's future."

—Henry Louis Gates, Jr.,
Alphonse Fletcher University Professor, Harvard University

"*Getting Smart about Race* promotes social understanding, drawing our attention to the peculiarly structural nature of systemic racism, while revealing some of its unlikely victims: white people. Gracefully written, accessible, and deeply illuminating—a reflexive work of singular importance that should be read and digested by everyone."

—Elijah Anderson, author of *The Cosmopolitan Canopy*

"Margaret Andersen's *Getting Smart about Race* is a road map for the substantive and constructive conversation about race we say we need to have. With the first sentence and one thoughtful question, she unsettles the racial landscape. . . . But she doesn't just discuss the problem, she offers a way for us to discover the shared humanity which must be the foundation for racial healing in the United States of America."

—Jeffrey Blount, Emmy Award–winning television director and
author of *The Emancipation of Evan Walls*

"In a clear, elegant, and thorough way, Margaret Andersen makes us all 'smart about race.' She tells us what race, racism, and prejudice are, their effects in society, and what we can do to change the racial order of things. *Getting Smart about Race* will help advance our national dialogue about the continuing significance of race."

—Eduardo Bonilla-Silva, Duke University;
author of *Racism without Racists*

"Like the cartoon fish who wonders what water is, white Americans are often oblivious to racism. This book is a necessary and timely corrective. Margaret Andersen has written an important examination of the 'water' that continues to stubbornly define and divide us. I strongly recommend it."

—Mark Bowden, journalist and author of
Black Hawk Down* and *The Last Stone

"Dr. Andersen's approach to conversations around racism is accessible to people of all backgrounds and provides a useful point of entry to discussions of race in a modern context. This book makes an important contribution to modern-day efforts to dismantle racism across the country."

—Kristen Clarke, president and executive director,
Lawyers' Committee for Civil Rights Under Law

"Margaret Andersen's clear, empathetic, evenhanded, and engaged writing can change the awareness of white readers who decide to face 'all of this talk about race.' Andersen makes their effort both worthwhile and rewarding. She lets readers know they matter and that what they think and do matters to the racial climate of this country—even the world. She shows us it is not too late to get smarter and outgrow what she calls the 'commonsense racism' of our childhood environments and educations. The humane tone of this book is a gift to all who are making efforts toward social justice in the United States."

—Peggy McIntosh, author of *Privilege, Fraudulence,*
***and Teaching As Learning* and founder of National**
SEED Project on Inclusive Curriculum
(Seeking Educational Equity and Diversity)

GETTING SMART ABOUT RACE

An American Conversation

MARGARET L. ANDERSEN

ROWMAN & LITTLEFIELD
Lanham • Boulder • New York • London

Published by Rowman & Littlefield
An imprint of The Rowman & Littlefield Publishing Group, Inc.
4501 Forbes Boulevard, Suite 200, Lanham, Maryland 20706
www.rowman.com

6 Tinworth Street, London SE11 5AL, United Kingdom

British Library Cataloguing in Publication Information Available

Library of Congress Cataloging-in-Publication Data

Names: Andersen, Margaret L., author.
Title: Getting Smart about Race : An American Conversation / Margaret L. Andersen.
Description: Lanham : Rowman & Littlefield, [2020] | Includes bibliographical references and index.
Identifiers: LCCN 2019042353 (print) | LCCN 2019042354 (ebook) | ISBN 9781538129494 (hardcover) | ISBN 9781538129500 (epub)
Subjects: LCSH: United States—Race relations. | Race discrimination—United States. | Equality—United States.
Classification: LCC E185.615 .A6793 2020 (print) | LCC E185.615 (ebook) | DDC 305.800973—dc23
LC record available at https://lccn.loc.gov/2019042353
LC ebook record available at https://lccn.loc.gov/2019042354

♾️™ The paper used in this publication meets the minimum requirements of American National Standard for Information Sciences—Permanence of Paper for Printed Library Materials, ANSI/NISO Z39.48-1992.

CONTENTS

Acknowledgments

Although my writing is a solo practice, I am nestled in an extended community of scholars, friends, and colleagues who make this work possible. There are so many people who have enthusiastically encouraged this book and who, in different ways, have supported what I do. I am deeply grateful to all those who at the very beginning said, "This is important; you should do it"; to those who provided heartfelt encouragement along the way; to those who commented on various ideas as I worked them out; and to those who read every word of the manuscript and gave extensive substantive and editorial criticisms. I thank every one of you for the part you played.

I especially thank Peggy Nelson and Maxine Baca Zinn, sister sociologists, who read every chapter and provided detailed commentary that has made this a better book. Gabrielle Cobb: I thank you for your early feedback and excitement that helped set the tone for reaching my intended audience. Suzanne Supplee, thank you for the detailed and exquisite editing, even when you were busy with your own writing and teaching. Michelle Asakawa and Laura Sanderson provided expert editorial eyes that also improved the book. I am fortunate to have a large circle of friends, each of whom played a special part as I wrote this book. Perhaps you read part of an early draft and cheered me on; maybe you passed on constant encouragement; perhaps you talked with me about your perspective on racism; maybe you helped enhance my social media platform; or maybe you were there for conversation, fun, friendship, and a glass of wine at the end of a writing day. You are all a critical part of my circle of support, so I graciously thank David Altenhofen, Jack and Carolyn Batty, Ralph Begleiter, David Breimhurst, Mariette Buchman, Patch Canada, Patricia DeLeon, Rich and Claudia Fischer, Valerie Hans, Elizabeth Higginbotham, Jane Hopkinson, Eve Howard, Suzie Hurley, Loren Kieve, Angela March, Tony Miksitz, Denise Nathanson, Amber and Mark Petry, Sara Robins, Amy Stein, Nancy Targett, Howard Taylor, and Beth Trujillo. Your contributions helped make this project possible.

I especially want to thank my family, whom I always count on for love and support. Thank you Arlene Hanerfeld, Norman Andersen, Kimball Johnson, Mary Brittain, Jessica Hanerfeld, Sarah Hanerfeld, Debbie and Jim Lanier, Aubrey Hanerfeld, and Aden Carcopo. It was really sad losing my mom, Emma Louise Johnson, while I was in the midst of this project, but I am so grateful for her love, her appreciation of my work, and the importance she gave to education over my entire life.

I also appreciate the work of the National Center for Faculty Development and Diversity (NCFDD) Faculty Success Program (FSP). The NCFDD team and my various FSP bootcamp groups provide structure, support, and accountability that keep me moving forward. Thank you as well to the staff and leadership of Morris Library at the University of Delaware for providing the resources that enable my work.

Rolf Janke, executive editor at Rowman & Littlefield, has been enthusiastic about this project from the beginning. I sincerely thank him for his encouragement and for shepherding this project through. Thank you as well to Courtney Packard, Jo-Ann Parks, Dina Giulak, and Janice Braunstein for the logistical support that took this book through production. I sincerely thank the publishing team at Rowman & Littlefield: Linda Ganster, Nancy Roberts, Jon Sisk, and Mark Kerr. You provided encouragement and some lighthearted fun in the middle of the hard work of writing. In these days of huge transformations in publishing, I appreciate your support for my work and your vision for sharing and transmitting ideas when so much is changing around us.

To my husband, Richard Morris Rosenfeld: You have been with me through so many writing projects and your love fills my days, even when I won't talk during writing time. You have listened patiently as I read sections of this book aloud; you read chapters, caught errors, discussed content, and encouraged me even when I was having doubts about being able to do this at all. I thank you for all of that and for the many years of steering our ship together.

Introduction

If the problem is fear, the answer is knowledge.
    —FORMER VICE PRESIDENT JOE BIDEN[1]

IN SOME WAYS, THERE HAS NEVER BEEN A MOMENT LIKE NOW IN our nation's racial history. In other ways, this is a moment repeated. Many were horrified when white nationalist Patrick Crusius shot and killed twenty-two people in El Paso, Texas, because he thought Latino immigrants were invading Texas. People were also shocked when the nation's president, Donald Trump, tweeted that four women of color in the US Congress—all of them US citizens and all but one born in the United States—should go back to the countries from which they allegedly came—African countries, one presumes.

Horrifying as it was, the El Paso massacre is not the first time that people of color have been killed because Whites saw them as a threat. In the aftermath of World War I, there was such an extensive wave of anti-Black riots across the nation's cities that the period between April and November 1919 was named "Red Summer." Hundreds of Black people were killed along with some Whites. Thousands of Black people had their lives disrupted, and fear gripped the nation. Additionally, the lynching of Mexican Americans in the American Southwest following the Mexican-American War of 1846–1848 was rampant, also based in fears about their threat to White people. The violence that ensued closely matches in frequency the lynching that terrorized Black Americans in the late nineteenth and early twentieth centuries.[2]

The old trope that tells people of color "to go back where they came from" has a long history in the United States, and Donald Trump is not the first president to mouth this racist sentiment. Abraham Lincoln, usually thought of as a champion of racial freedom, advocated that Black Americans should go back to Africa. In his words, "The separation of the races is the only perfect preventative of amalgamation. . . . Let us be brought to believe it is morally right, and, at the same time, favorable to, or, at least not against our interest to transfer the African to his native clime, and we shall find a way to do it."[3] Over the years, including now, countless Black Americans, Chinese Americans, Muslim Americans, Mexican and Central Americans, and other people from diverse backgrounds have been told to "go back where they came from"—as if America were not a land of multiple people from multiple origins. The assumption, even if a tacit one, seems to be that the United States is supposed to be "white"—even though whiteness is itself a mix of national origins and ethnicities.

Perhaps the recent events of racial hatred have shocked the nation because so many people somehow thought we were "beyond race." After all, the nation elected its first African American president, Barack Obama, and the value of "diversity" has become so commonly extolled that it has practically lost its meaning. Racist incidents have, nonetheless, continued to appear on the national news. Whenever such an event occurs, media pundits and members of the public bandy about opinions as to who is a racist and who is not, as if ferreting out racism is just a matter of identifying racist individuals and either changing or silencing them. This assumption, though, misses the point that racism is more than individual attitudes. Racism is built into society and can be present even when it is not overtly expressed.

People are confused about racism, as if it is only present when it flares up in its overt forms or when racism is directly observed in particular comments or behaviors. But racism comes in many forms, not all of which can be seen clearly. Just because someone claims not to "see" race or says nothing explicitly racial does not mean that racism is absent. Getting smart about race means recognizing how racism is built into society, calling it out for what it is, and then doing something to change it.

The recent resurgence of overt and public acts of racism demands that we do so. Getting smarter about race is as urgent now as it has ever been. All-too-frequent police shootings of Black people;* neo-Nazi marches; the slaughter of Jewish worshippers in synagogues; holding Latino immigrants at the southern border in cages; references to immigrants as "vermin" and "an infestation"; proposals to exclude Muslims from entering the nation: These and many other examples have made the reality of racial hatred and injustice jarring and deeply disturbing. Moreover, by the time this book is published, there are likely to be other such horrid examples.

Acts of racial hatred demand our attention, especially now as many people are shocked by the resurgence of racism in its ugliest forms. You will hear some people say, "I just can't believe this is happening now." Or, "We really need to understand this." Yet at the same time there is surprisingly little in-depth public discussion about race and racism, especially among White people. Just mention race or racism and people—White people particularly—become nervous, defensive, possibly even angry. White people fear saying something wrong or, worse, being called a racist. They might then remain silent. Silence, though, leads to acquiescence, reproducing racial inequality. Still, racial stereotypes and prejudicial statements flare up all too easily. Although people of color talk frequently about race among themselves, in mixed-race company, they fear being ignored, hurt, or insulted. In the end, frank and informed discussions about race and racism are rare, although sorely needed. As common as racism is in our everyday lives, it is

---

* *Black* and *White* are capitalized in this book to reflect that they are people's named identities. See the "Note on Language" at the end of this introduction for further discussion of how language is used in this book.

seldom seriously analyzed, even though it is one of the most critical issues of the day.

With this book, I hope to inspire more conversations about race and racism—conversations (public and private) informed by sound research, not just by strong opinion or racial stereotypes. As someone who has been studying and teaching about racial inequality in the United States for many years, I am convinced that a better-informed public can move our nation toward a more racially just society.

I also know that discussions about race can be discomforting—no matter one's own place in the current system of racial inequality. Some years ago, while talking about American race relations, a young White man said to me, "You are making me very uncomfortable."

"Why?" I queried.

"Because you are making me question things I thought were true." I think about that moment often. I probably said something in return like, "Being uncomfortable and challenging what you think are the main reasons for educating yourself about race." I still believe that. Being uncomfortable when confronted with new ideas is how we learn, especially about difficult and sensitive social issues. For many of us, there may be nothing so discomforting as thinking about and acting to change race and racism.

I know from my years of teaching and from my own background that education matters. I want this book to provide the general public with an accessible overview of what we know about racial inequality—what race is (and is not); the impact of racism on people's daily lives; and how our attitudes and beliefs are shaped by prejudice and racism. But I also want people to understand that racism is about more than individual attitudes, as important as these are. Racial inequality is built into our society and is manifested in every aspect of our social institutions—workplaces, schools, neighborhoods, health care, the criminal justice system, and more. Yet, popular ideas about race continue to blame those most victimized by it—ideas I hope are debunked by the research that informs this book.

In the end, I want a more informed understanding to help us know what to do about racial inequality in the United States. I am certainly not the only person to argue for or desire this. There are many whose writing and activism informs my own conclusions. What I want is a far-reaching national conversation that can guide social change—in our individual beliefs and practices, in our communities, and in our social policies.

As a White woman who grew up in very different racial environments, I have had to face my own discomforts as I learned about race and racism. I was born in Oakland, California—and the minute I tell people that, I typically encounter some horrible racial stereotype about Oakland as a "black" city. In 1958, when I was ten years old, my family moved from Oakland into the heart of Jim Crow segregation—to Rome, Georgia. As a young girl moving into a new place, I wanted desperately just to "fit in," and I tried hard to be accepted in what seemed like a strange new environment. Even though I was from California, I was quickly labeled a "Yankee"—something I thought referred only to people from New England! As an outsider, I was keenly aware of the bizarre norms of Jim Crow racism, such as how much it suddenly mattered where I sat on the bus. I was once reprimanded by my grandmother for rushing to a seat in the far back of the bus—my favorite place to sit when we lived in California. I was very alert to the norms of racial segregation—the fact that there were separate schools for White and "colored" people; separate drinking fountains; separate neighborhoods for White and Black people; and strong social conventions about how you should speak to people, including to the domestic workers who seemed to be working in most White homes. I was, however, too sheltered in my White world—clueless, you might say—to understand what I now know as the gross inhumanity of this oppressive racial regime. To this day, as I read about the period when I grew up, I continue to

INTRODUCTION

discover there was a very different world in Rome, Georgia, than the White one I was absorbed in. Invisible to me at the time was a world of Black achievement against the odds, strong family values within the Black community, simmering Black resistance, and legal challenges that were to transform the world I lived in.

After a few years in Rome, in 1961 my family moved to Boston. I saw again how pervasive racism was—even in the supposedly more liberal North. There were very few Black students in my school in suburban Arlington, Massachusetts—none in my academic classes. My neighborhood was just as White as the one in Georgia, although people of Italian descent were a novelty to me. I do not recall interacting with any Black people while living in the Boston suburbs.

When we returned to Georgia for my last two years of high school, segregation was finally being dismantled, although only in the smallest ways. In 1966, my high school was forced to integrate by court order—a full twelve years after the *Brown v. Board of Education* Supreme Court decision. Four Black students were admitted to my senior class of about one hundred twenty-five. I still remember the uproar among White friends—especially their parents—when there was a chance a Black male student might hold my White friend's hand at the annual teen talent show. Her mother was so horrified by this possibility that she forced my friend to withdraw from the pageant. The young man went on to become a Stanford graduate, a practicing attorney, and—later—a seventh-grade math teacher; math had always been his passion. I cannot claim to have understood all the ramifications of racism when I was in high school, but I remember thinking things were very wrong in my school, in my town, and, indeed, in my country. Perhaps these early experiences led me to study racial inequality in the United States. Who knows? Certainly, the social movements of the 1960s awakened my consciousness—and in a big way. Little did I know then I would devote myself later to learning, teaching, and writing about racial inequality in America.

As I write this book, the United States still faces the many horrors of racism. They are different from when I grew up, but just as damaging. Unlike the Black-White divide that marked my early years, race has become even more complicated as Latinos/as, Asian Americans, Native Americans, and Muslim Americans have become more visible and vocal—and a larger proportion of the US population. Although for a time it seemed, at least to some, that the United States was becoming a more color-blind society, we now see that the old era of overt racism has changed, but never left. Covert forms of racism are maddeningly common, but overt racism has also been on the rise. Hardly a day goes by without news of another overtly racist incident—a word I use hesitatingly because "incident" so trivializes the experience of racism. The presence of both overt and covert racism tells us that racial inequality endures as a definitive feature of US society.

You need not be an expert in social science to observe the stubborn reality of race in the United States. The evidence is compelling:

- The income gap between Black and White families in the United States has remained virtually unchanged since 1970 (at about 60 percent). While the income gap is large and unchanging, the wealth gap between Blacks and Whites is even more startling. On average, White Americans have twelve times the wealth of Black Americans and ten times as much as Hispanic Americans.

- Even in a so-called good economy, when unemployment is low, African Americans, and now Latinos, have twice the rate of unemployment of White Americans. Furthermore, this ratio has not budged over time. Among Black and Hispanic youth, rates of unemployment and joblessness are staggering—and bode poorly for these young people's future life prospects.

- Despite periodic claims that poverty has ended, one-quarter of African American people and one-fifth of Hispanics live below the poverty line, compared to 9 and 11 percent of non-Hispanic Whites and Asians, respectively. Fully one-third of Black children and nearly one-third of Hispanic children live below the federally defined poverty line.

Given that the United States is a relatively affluent society, these facts are infuriating. In the face of these facts, how can we explain—and thus change—the racial inequality that pervades society? One book cannot completely answer that question, but it can provide an informed perspective about the origins and consequences of this most obstinate social reality.

The first chapter of this book discusses the concept of race, including its origins and the myth of biological race. As the chapter title suggests, race is a thoroughly social idea—developed to allegedly explain the gross exploitation of certain human groups. Chapter 2 explores how racism feels, especially in how the everyday experience of racism shapes the mental and physical health of people of color. As you will see, racism also affects White people—and diminishes our capacity for a fully realized human society. For White readers, this chapter also lays some groundwork for building empathy—a theme reappearing in the final chapter. Chapter 3 distinguishes prejudice and racism and shows the limitations of thinking of racism purely as a matter of individual attitudes. Chapter 4 debunks some of the common beliefs stemming from racism, especially how commonsense beliefs about race deflect people's attention from the reality of racial inequality. Chapter 5 explores how past actions and policies continue to influence current patterns of racial advantage and disadvantage. The final chapter discusses what we can do to reduce racial inequality—both as individuals and in broader social policies and organizations. The two appendices in the book provide resources for people who want to further engage these issues—resources than can stimulate discussion in workplaces, schools, and community organizations.

The first appendix, "Finding Common Ground: Questions for Conversation," includes discussion questions that can be used in organizations and community groups to help people who want to think about what they can do to reduce racism in society. The second appendix provides a list of suggested books, films, and videos that can be used for further education about race.

A NOTE ON LANGUAGE

Words can hurt, and language is fraught with racial meaning. Any book on race then must be attentive to the words and labels it uses. What we call people, how we say it, whose voice is active and whose passive: All these practices connote racial meanings. While writing this book, I was keenly aware of how word choice conveys particular meanings about race, including what people are called. In a society where race carries so much weight, I want to make my choices involving words and labels clear and provide my reasons for using the words I do.

Labeling racial groups inevitably oversimplifies people's identities and risks making race seem to be intractable. Although the US population is often grouped into five major categories—White, Black (or African American), Latino/a (or Hispanic), Asian American, and Native American—each of these groups is highly diverse, complex in their identities, and neither fixed nor immutable over time. I realize that some groups generally included in these labels, such as the label *Latino*, object to being called so. The label *Latino* is an aggregated term that is meant to convey common experiences and linked interests, but it also hides people's specific identities as Chicano/a, Mexicano, Puerto Rican, Guatemalan, and so forth. General labels cloak specific identities but there is no way to generalize about group experiences without using these aggregated terms. I have not used the term *Latinx*, now proposed as a way of abolishing the gender binary in the use of Latino and Latina. There is a lively debate within the Latino community about the term Latinx—some saying it disrespects traditional cultural values, others arguing for the elimination of gender distinctions. In the end, I have to live with these many language dilemmas—trying to be respectful of individual identities, but also being sociological in analyzing group experiences.

In reporting data from federal agencies or others' research, I have used the terms found in the original source. In the census, for example, those terms are typically non-Hispanic White, Black (or African American), Hispanic, and Asian American, and, sometimes, multiracial. There is maddeningly little data on Native Americans collected as part of routine surveys in many of these sources and, thus, Native Americans are often omitted in some of the government data here, especially as presented in charts and other descriptive data.

I have capitalized White and Black throughout the book to reflect that they are people's named identities. For some this may appear jarring; for others, it is now common practice. The term *White* itself is fraught with political meaning, as new studies of whiteness are finding. Certainly, not all Whites share the same advantages as the White population writ large. You will note, for reasons elaborated in chapter 1, that I never use the term *Caucasian* because of its racist origins—even though it is widespread as a label in US culture.

I have found it impossible to avoid the term *minority* when referring to racial and ethnic groups who experience discrimination in US society. Many now object to this term because people of color are becoming a numerical majority in the United States. In many places, they already are. When used here, however, minority is used in the sociological sense of the term—that is, to refer to groups that share common historical and cultural experiences of prejudice and discrimination. In other words, minority refers to an experience, not a number or proportion.

Likewise, I have used race in a way that encapsulates ethnicity. Some will object to this, knowing that ethnicity, not race, is what defines many people's experiences, and not all so-called racial groups share the same ethnic background. Jewish people, Muslim Americans, and Latinos are, for example, not "races," and African Americans, usually thought of as a "race," have quite diverse ethnic backgrounds. Still, many ethnic groups face *racialization* (as in Latinos being defined as "brown")—a concept you will learn in the first chapter. In the end, although race is not "real," racism is. When any group is treated with racial hatred, whether that is based on religion, cultural practices, national origin, or any other group characteristic, ethnicity can be understood in the context of racial dynamics.

In sum, language reflects the political and social status of diverse groups and people. I have tried to avoid any language that insults or belittles people, even if unintentionally. We also know that language shapes people's perceptions of reality. Being attentive to the language of race can help reduce racism. The language here may not always be perfect and, as has happened before, language about race and ethnicity is likely to change. I only ask that readers pay attention to the language they use, understanding that language reflects power relationships and is an important part of the path to greater racial equality.

CHAPTER 1

Race

A Thoroughly Social Idea

Race is a pigment of the imagination.

—RUBÉN RUMBAUT[1]

SUPPOSE FOR JUST A MINUTE THAT YOU COULD CHANGE YOUR RACE —that is, wake up tomorrow morning only to learn that by some amazing feat, you had been switched from White to African American or Latino to Asian or African American to White. What would change? Perhaps you might say, "Nothing," believing that people are all alike. Perhaps you would be concerned that your income level would drop—or maybe it would go up. Who would be around you at work or in school? Would your friends change? Your neighborhood? Perhaps you would find that people looked at you differently based on your looks. What rights would people like you have had over time?

Such an exercise is not as imaginary as you might think. It is precisely what happened to Susie Phipps, a Louisiana woman who lived most of her life thinking she was White, only to find out—by a quirk—that she was officially noted as "Black."* Susie Phipps grew up White, never thinking of herself in any other way. Born

---

* See "A Note on Language" in the introduction to understand why *Black* and *White* are capitalized in this book.

Susie Guillory in Louisiana in 1934, she married Andy Phipps (a White man) in 1977. When the couple applied for passports so they could travel to South America, the state of Louisiana told Susie Phipps that her birth certificate recorded both her parents as "col"—that is, colored—or Black, even though her children's birth certificates listed her and her two children as "White." According to the law, she was therefore Black. She tried to change her birth certificate to reflect what she believed as her true identity—that is, White—but the state would not budge.

As it turns out, Susie Guillory Phipps's great-great-great-great-grandmother (named Marguerite) was a Black slave—five generations back. When Phipps applied for her passport, the laws in Louisiana defined anyone with a trace of Black ancestry as "Black." Susie Phipps sued the state of Louisiana to have her birth certificate changed, but in 1983, she lost her case. The law was not overturned until years later.

Louisiana was not unique among southern states in defining a person's race by the *one drop rule*—that is, the practice of defining someone as "Black" if they had any Black ancestry. States varied in the particulars. Mississippi classified someone as "Black" if they had "any appreciable amount of Negro blood." North Carolina, Florida, and Texas defined Black as anyone having one-eighth Black ancestry.

Oddly enough, at the time of Phipps's case, you might be defined as a given race in one state and a different race in another. In Virginia, even as late as 1963, you were considered Indian if you lived on a reservation and had at least one American Indian grandparent. Off the reservation, you would be considered Black. Your official identity could even change over time within a given state. In Virginia in 1785 any person with "one-fourth part or more Negro blood" was deemed a "colored" person, but in 1910, the percentage was changed to one-sixteenth. Later, in 1924, the Virginia Racial Purity Act decreed that having *any trace* of African ancestry meant you were Black, as if one could somehow measure such a thing!

Why would there be such variation—and strict oversight—in how race is defined? Most of these state laws were not passed until early in the twentieth century—at a time often referred to as the "golden age of racism." Following the Civil War and Reconstruction, the nation was undergoing major changes in race relations. Whites rushed to reinstate the earlier racial order. State governments passed laws to strictly regulate social relations and to define who counted as a citizen. Citizenship then determined who could own property, vote, and marry. In other words, racial designations were created to regulate the basic rights of citizenship—who had them and who did not. Likewise, as is now well known, when it was written, the US Constitution counted Black slaves as only three-fifths of a person for purposes of determining state representation in Congress. Defining race has been a core component in building America's basic institutions.

The laws that historically defined race may seem antiquated to you now, but their legacy lives on. Race is no longer defined as it once was. People no longer think of race in terms of some percentage of "blood," but they do still think of skin color as a presumed marker of race. Who do people think of as White or Black and what groups become defined as "a race?" Latinos—even in all their diversity—are ethnic groups, defined by their common culture and heritage, but many are becoming racialized—that is, becoming defined as "Brown" people. As you will learn in this book, race is not decided by individual attributes, such as skin color or other physical characteristics. Rather, *race is a social construction*. That is, the meaning of race—and how that meaning develops and changes over time and in different contexts—is a matter of socially generated ideas, not just one's individual identity.

Saying race is a social construction does not mean that race is any less "real" or that a person's racial identity is not important. Quite the contrary, how race is defined has consequences—both for individuals and for groups as a whole. In fact, it has enormous consequences. In societies organized around racial ideas—as is certainly the case in the United States—race determines all manner of things, ranging from how people relate to each other to how resources in society are distributed. The very idea of race stems from social ideas—ideas that themselves come from how different people are treated in society. Seeing race as a social construction means thinking about it not as an individual attribute, but as a social process. Race is generated and sustained in society. This means that transforming race relations must involve societal, not just individual, change.

THE MYTH OF BIOLOGICAL RACE

You might ask, doesn't one's race come from biological characteristics? The current popularity of DNA test kits might lead you to think your race can be found in your genes. DNA testing is now widely available to anyone willing to pay a relatively small amount of money to trace their genetic ancestry. Indeed, DNA test kit companies promise to send you the secret to your "true" identity— perhaps finding lost relatives or discovering some unknown ethnic ancestry. DNA is now commodified and sold. Put more graphically, as sociologist Jonathan Marks writes, genetics has become a "cash cow."[2] The kits and other forms of DNA testing of course have many benefits: screening for genetically linked diseases, possibly freeing wrongly convicted prisoners, or locating a long-lost relative. But do they reveal your "true identity"?

Answering this question requires some basic understanding of genetics and the current science of DNA testing. Scientists are now able to map the entire human genome—that is, the full sequence of human DNA, including the twenty-three pairs of chromosomes that encode our genetic identity. The *genotype* of any organism, including humans, is the specific gene combination that an individual has for expressing a trait. The full set of genes found in an organism is the genome. The *phenotype*, on the other hand, refers to *observable* characteristics, such as what you look like.

Although many people think that genes "cause" certain outcomes, few genetic traits are directly expressed. Take blood type—a genetic trait: A person is either type A, B, AB, or O depending on the genotype makeup. But most observable characteristics in human beings—that is, their phenotype—fall along a continuum, with *both* inherited characteristics *and* the environment influencing the actual expression of the human trait. Height is a good example. You might inherit the tendency to be tall or short, but your environment will significantly affect your actual height. Scientists know that complex human traits (such as intelligence, artistic talent, and even such basic biological facts as one's height) are clearly influenced by the environment—in other words, human culture.

It would be stupid to ignore the fact that people look different based on what we think of as race. In various societies, skin color distinguishes different groups, including how people perceive and treat each other. Of course, there are identifiable physical differences among human populations. Some of those physical characteristics are produced by the action of our genes. Genes also interact with each other. Scientists currently estimate three or four gene pairs determine skin color. Skin color, however, is a phenotypic trait, partially based on inherited genes but also influenced by environmental factors.

Most people do not understand the complexity that geneticists are now discovering. The mass media routinely oversimplify research studies about genetics, leading the public to think there is a direct causal relationship between particular genes and a given condition. This is generally not true. For example, there are correlations between genes and particular diseases, but this does not necessarily mean that genes are causal determinants of disease. Health and disease are influenced by all kinds of social factors, including lifestyle, access to quality health care, and diet—all social and environmental factors, not genetically determined ones.

Although there may be some genetic influence on race-based traits, none of the traits used to define race (skin color, hair texture, and so forth) correspond to true genetic differences between human populations. Unlike in the animal kingdom where you can separate animals into distinct species, there is only one species of human beings. You simply cannot separate people into discrete, supposedly "racial" categories based on their genetic makeup or, for that matter, based on the color of their skin.

Using genetic information, you can tell some things about an individual's ancestry, but you cannot do the opposite—that is, infer something about what someone is like given their ancestry. But we do this all the time. Just think of all the stereotypes associated with different ancestral groups: You might learn, for example, that you have some American Indian ancestry, but does this make you Indian? Or just because you have some Scandinavian ancestry, does this make you blond? As the medical scientist and physician Siddhartha Mukherjee states, "Every genome carries a signature of an individual's ancestry, but an individual's racial ancestry predicts little about the person's genome."[3] You might learn from a DNA kit that you have ancestry in Sierra Leone or as an American Indian, but this tells you nothing about who you actually are. Still, people make all kinds of assumptions based on what they perceive as a person's race and ethnicity. *The power of race comes not from genetic information but from the social stereotypes that notions of race have created.*

Scientists now know that there are far more genetic similarities among people than there are differences. As the adage says, "We are all the same inside." Biologically speaking, if you take any two people (including two people from supposedly different races) and analyze their genetic composition, you will find they are more alike than different. The fact is that genetic variation among human beings is indeed very small. In fact, 99.9 percent of the genetic code is identical in all human beings. Put differently, a mere one-tenth of one percent of the three billion rungs on the DNA chain varies across different human beings. The vast proportion of genetic diversity occurs *within* so-called racial groups, not across them.

This is a very important point for anyone who thinks race is a biological given or who makes claims about some genetic trait causing some presumed race-based behavior. Even so-called racial traits (such as skin color or hair texture) do not exist in discrete categories—a condition that would be needed to take any species and divide it into so-called racial groups. Scientists have soundly concluded that *there is no such thing as a race gene.* The genetic truth is that we are far more alike than we are different and there is more variation within so-called racial groups than there is across such groups.

RACE: A QUITE MODERN IDEA

If our race is not determined exclusively by biology, where does race come from? Ideas about race have not always been with us and they have very specific origins in Western culture. Even though race is known *not* to be found in our biology, this truth has not stopped people over the years from trying to categorize people into so-called race groups.

Various people have created many different schemes for dividing human beings into races. At one time, some thought that earwax could be used as a "marker" of race.[4] In the 1950s, many schoolchildren were taught that there were four races in the world—white, black, red, and Mongoloid (whatever that was). And over the years, anthropologists and others have devised hundreds of schemes in attempts to classify human beings into racial groups. One of the most egregious examples of "race making" was the Nazi regime in Germany when Hitler created the alleged "Aryan" race (that is, blond, blue-eyed people who he thought were superior to everyone else). This creation of a supposedly superior race was, as we now know, done in an effort to eradicate millions of Jewish people.

Schemes to define race may seem obsolete now, yet they still resonate in how people think about race. White people now routinely identify themselves as "Caucasian," never wondering what this term means or where it came from. Would you ever have imagined this term comes from one man who over two hundred years ago developed a scheme for the "types" of human beings?

Johann Friedrich Blumenbach (1752–1841) was a German physician and naturalist. Like other naturalists of the time, Blumenbach believed you could create a taxonomy of human types. Such taxonomies were common then as many men (and they were men), believing they were doing scientific work, developed various ways to organize human beings into hierarchies of presumed "races." Johann Blumenbach thought there were five separate "varieties" of human beings: Caucasian, Mongolian, Ethiopian, American, and Malay. He was particularly smitten with the people of the Russian Caucasus, who were mostly blond and light-skinned, and who he believed were the most beautiful people in the world. He placed "Caucasians" at the "top" of his alleged racial hierarchy of human beings. That is how the term *Caucasian*, still with us today, appeared.

Although Blumenbach's ideas seem outlandish to us now, the endurance of the Caucasian label shows how intractable racist thinking of the past is—even today. Maybe you will cringe the next time you hear someone identify herself as "Caucasian" or you will think twice if you check "Caucasian" in a box to indicate your race. Typically, no one questions this designation now and few know its origins, but its origins reveal how deep the vein of racial thinking lies—even in the everyday language of race.

The idea that human beings can be separated into races corresponds closely with the development of social systems that have exploited some people for the profit of others, namely, slavery. Indeed, the schemes that have been developed throughout history reflect far more about the racial politics and social systems of the time than they reflect any true scientific facts. The idea that humans can be divided into so-called races only makes sense within the context of a system of racial inequality. Why? Exploiting a particular group, as happened under slavery, could only be "explained" (at least by the dominant group) if the group being oppressed was defined as something less than fully human. As slavery spread throughout the Western world, the idea of race was created to justify the cruel institution of slavery. Various racial taxonomies were created as the Atlantic slave trade flourished in the eighteenth and nineteenth centuries. The Dutch, Spanish, and British empires colonized much of the world—for purposes of trade and the acquisition of wealth. Human trafficking was pivotal to this system. As this global economic system emerged, the world was ripe for the scourge of racism. It is no coincidence that ideas about innate human differences were developed to purportedly justify the development of an institutionalized system of slavery in North and South America. Slavery depended on classifying some groups as innately inferior to Europeans. Only if some people could be considered something less than fully human could a system of racial subordination emerge.

Ironically, the racism that emerged in the eighteenth century developed alongside Western movements for democracy, namely the French and American revolutions. How could aspirations for equality go hand in hand with racism? As people were rejecting old notions of the traditional order, the dominant class had to have some explanation to justify the exploitation and mistreatment of others. In the thinking of the most powerful group, if differences between two groups who are unequal were defined as "natural," then there would be no need to question racial inequality. The idea of race filled that need.

The racism we live with now, though perpetuated through contemporary social institutions and ideas, has its origins in older forms of exploitation. Moreover, those origins are relatively recent in human history. At its heart, racism is the idea that there are distinct groups of human beings, some of whom are superior to others. Most people no longer think of race as a biological given, nor do most outwardly believe that people can be classified into different racial groups. But when you unpack how racism operates, it comes down to a simple, though wrong-headed, idea: the idea that some people are superior to others. Keep in mind that this idea emerged in the context of grotesque human oppression.

CLASSIFYING RACE: WHO COUNTS

Once you understand that society creates the concept of race, you realize that race is a social construction. Questions then emerge, such as *who* defines race and *how*. How do official designations of race match people's racial identities—or not? Where does the concept of race come from? Laws can define race, as was the case of Suzie Phipps that opened this chapter. Now, race is also defined through various organizational rules, regulations, and instructions, such as on census forms, your driver's license, employment applications, college admissions applications, medical records, and countless other bureaucratic forms.

The US Constitution requires the federal government to enumerate the US population every ten years. How the census has classified people into presumed racial groups and how these classifications have changed over the years shows us just how socially constructed race is. The earliest years of the census simply counted people as either "white," "free colored," or "slave." In 1850 the government added the category "mulatto." Indians were not counted at all until 1860. In 1860 "Chinese" and "Asian Indian" were added to the census classifications. "Japanese" was added in 1870.

Racial designations changed again in 1900. At that time, you would be classified by the census as White, Black, Indian, Japanese or Chinese, or mulatto; *Other* appeared in 1910. In 1930 *Mexican, Hindu, Korean*, and *Filipino* were added to census designations. From 1940 to 1960 the census took little note of race, classifying people as either *White* or *Negro*. Oddly enough, until 1960 a person's race was based solely on the census taker's observation. By 1960 the US Census Bureau started collecting more information about race, largely as a result of political pressure from civil rights leaders who saw a careful enumeration as essential for the fair distribution of federal resources and data collection on discrimination. Later, in 1980, the census added a designation for Hispanic origin, at the urging of Latino activists.

In 2000 the federal government once again modified its racial designations to include White; Black; American Indian and Alaska Native; Asian; Native Hawaiian and other Pacific Islander. And in 2000, for the first time the census added a separate check box for "Hispanic origin." By checking a separate box for Hispanic identity, Hispanics could be included as any race (that is, Black, White, or any of the other racial categories) while also being counted as Hispanic.

Starting with the 2000 census, a person could also check more than one box, thus allowing people to identify as multiracial. These shifting categories make analyzing census data over time a very complicated matter and some of the older categories seem really odd now. How these racial and ethnic categories change over time, however, follows a racial logic that might not make sense in and of itself but reflects the political and social context of the time, as well as the fact that various interest groups assert what influence they can on how the census enumerates the population.

Census designations will change again with the 2020 census. If the planned questions hold, the census will continue to ask two questions, one about race and one about ethnicity. Hispanics will continue to be classified in terms of ethnicity—everyone else as a "race." As in the past, the final designations will result from a contested and highly political process. Lebanese- and Egyptian-origin Americans will be classified as *White*; Ethiopians, Somalis, and Haitians as *Black or African Americans*. Native Hawaiians will be classified as a race, as will Asian Indians, Vietnamese, Japanese Americans, and others.

The reasons that these designations matter—and why they are so contested—is that the census enumerations determine representation in Congress through how political districts are drawn.

Census enumerations are also the basis for the distribution of various federal benefits, including how much different communities receive for such things as hospitals, roads, and other public goods. Businesses also use census data to make decisions about where to locate offices, factories, and other commercial establishments. Undercounting certain groups—a perennial problem for the census—means that people in some areas are not as well represented in government and receive fewer federal and state resources. Because people of color are more likely to be undercounted, policies about who counts and how can result in furthering racial disadvantage.

In other words, counting and classifying people really matters. Without good census data, social scientists would be crippled in their ability to document and monitor information about the lives and experiences of American people. Accurate data about the racial composition of the population is critical for documenting and monitoring racial discrimination, just as gender composition is important for monitoring gender discrimination. Although you might think we should abandon the concept of race altogether, how people are counted and classified is critical for these reasons.

As the United States has become more multiracial and multicultural, counting and classifying race has become more complex, and more controversial, than ever. Why would Native Hawaiians be considered a racial group, but not Hispanics? Why are some groups classified as "White," while others from the same continent are classified under "Black?" How would someone with a Puerto Rican and an Asian parent complete the census form? Are Mexican Americans a race? Under what social and historical conditions might they be considered such? Do the available categories match people's own identities? Why or why not? Trying to answer these questions shows how complicated—and political—defining race is. The very meaning of race changes over time. In other words, the concept of race is a thoroughly social idea.

MAKING RACE: RACE AS IDENTITY

The meaning of race is not just a matter of official designations—what Matthew Snipp calls administrative definitions of race.[5] Race is a crucial fact of people's identity—more than just a check-off box. It can be a source of pride, ancestry, collective history, and a sense of belonging to a community. Still, the meaning of race can only be understood in the context of society. Racial identity is, however, more important to some people than others, again reflecting the fact that race only takes on meaning in the context of society. You can see this with a simple experiment.

Write down, as quickly as you can, as many answers as you can to this question: "Who am I?" Your answers are likely to reflect the most prominent parts of your identity. Perhaps you answered: mother; student; American; woman; son; or your occupational status. Chances are that if you are African American, Latino, Asian, or Native American, you included that identity in your list. If you are White, you probably did not include that on your list of significant identities. This is because being White is usually taken for granted, not seen by White people as somehow relevant to who they are. But if you are, for example, African American, that identity was probably quite close to the top of your list.

This question and the resulting answers are part of a social psychological experiment known as the Twenty Statements Test. First developed in the 1950s, the Twenty Statements Test has been used to study people's most salient identities. Theoretically, the more important a particular identity is, the more likely someone will list it and the closer that identity will be to the top of the list. Researchers find that people in racial or ethnic minority groups almost always mention their race and mention it near the top of their list. White people rarely do either.

If you are White, do you think of yourself as having a race? Perhaps you do, although it is not likely to be something that you think about very often. People of color certainly think of you as White: It is likely one of the first things they note when meeting you. White people are not very conscious of their racial status and can take it for granted in a society where whiteness brings certain privileges and advantages. When in a setting where most others are people of color, White people become highly aware of their racial status. Of course, not all White people are alike, but the value of being white accrues to a person whether the person is aware of it or not.

Like other forms of racial identity, "whiteness" is a social construction. At times in our nation's history, whiteness has been defined through law. Such was the case for Takao Ozawa. Born in Japan in 1875, Takao Ozawa immigrated to San Francisco in 1894 as a nineteen-year-old young man. He graduated from a US high school, attended the University of California–Berkeley, and then moved to Hawaii, where he worked for an American company and raised a family. But when he applied to become a naturalized citizen, he was denied. He argued in court that he was a model citizen and fully assimilated into American life. He also argued that his skin was "lighter" than that of many White Americans. His case ultimately went to the US Supreme Court, but in 1922 the Court denied Ozawa the right to citizenship, arguing that he was not Caucasian.

The Ozawa case shows how whiteness can be constructed at the "macro" level of society—in his case, through the law. Race, however, can also be constructed at the "micro" level of identity—that is, through one's own self-definition or the definitions others have of you. Either way—macro or micro—race is constructed. You might think about Ozawa's case as you think about the status of people now known as "DREAMers," who came to the United States as very young children when their parents were not legal immigrants. How have they been constructed in racial terms? Have they been constructed as "brown," as somehow "not white?" How is this affecting their rights to citizenship? Such an example shows you how powerful the social construction of race can be in determining basic human rights and in shaping our individual identities.

You might also recall the case of Rachel Dolezal, a White woman with no known Black or African ancestry, who pretended to be Black and served as president of the Spokane, Washington, chapter of the National Association for the Advancement of Colored People (NAACP)—the prominent civil rights organization. The revelation that she was, in fact, "White" triggered a national controversy. When her white identity was discovered, she was removed from the NAACP leadership position and fired from her position as a faculty member in Africana Studies at Eastern Washington University. Both African American and White people accused her of falsifying her identity, though Dolezal continued to insist that she was "Black." Following the national scandal, she even changed her name to Nkechi Amare Diallo, claiming that her notoriety as Rachel Dolezal would prevent her from ever getting a job. What a bizarre twist—to change your name to an apparently African name to avoid discrimination!

The national controversy that ensued over Dolezal's case showed the intensity of people's feelings about racial identity. Many were furious that Dolezal could claim to be Black even while benefiting from a lifetime of being White. Some also argued that her making race appear to be a choice minimized the actual experience of living as a Black person in America. As a visibly light-skinned person, Dolezal could avoid the consequences that anyone with dark skin would face regardless of how they might identify. This case reveals the enormous power that "race" holds over us, even while being a socially manufactured idea.

Race, for example, can also be imposed on you by others. The definition of Jewish people as a "race" in Nazi Germany and the construction of Hitler's so-called Aryan race is the classic example—one that resulted in the systematic murder of millions of Jewish people, along with others. Even without this extreme example, you can imagine situations where race is imposed. For example, during their initial immigration to the United States, Irish people were defined as "black." Sometimes, people might even be accused of "not being black enough" or "selling out" if the person does not exhibit certain attitudes and behaviors associated with "blackness." "Passing" has also historically been a way that some light-skinned Black people constructed themselves as White in order to escape racial discrimination—an effort that typically required great secrecy, perhaps separation from one's own family and community, and extraordinary psychic cost.

Sociologists Aliya Saperstein and Andrew Penner have also shown in a clever experiment how racial attitudes of the time can construct race, especially in the judgments people make about others. Saperstein and Penner asked interviewers to classify a person's race based on certain characteristics of the person's life. Even without seeing pictures of people, interviewers were much more likely to classify a person as "Black" if the person was unemployed, on welfare, poor, or incarcerated—all current stereotypes about Black people. Interviewers were more likely to classify someone as White if they were married or living in the suburbs.

This research and the other examples above show how one's social status and the social attitudes of the time actually define race—both in interpersonal interaction and, at times, in legal decisions. Once again, we see that the concept of race—and the consequences of that social construction—originate in social behaviors, not the actual attributes of particular people.

RACIALIZING "OTHERS": WHO GETS TO BE WHITE?

You can see from the preceding discussion that *race is a process, not a thing*. It is a process that involves official policies, such as the law and other state-based rules and regulations, but also emerges from how you perceive yourself and how others see you. Race can also be imposed by powerful people, and in some cases, might be individually chosen. However defining race happens, society and its systems of power are usually involved.

Sociologists use the term *racialization* to describe the process by which groups come to be thought of in racial terms. Groups may become *racialized* not because of some inherent characteristic of the group, but because of their position in a racial hierarchy. You can see this happening now to some groups in the United States. Latinos are a good example. Some Latinos are becoming racialized because of their position in society. Latinos have very diverse cultural origins and different groups vary in their overall social and economic status. Indeed, some Latinos are even be perceived as White, especially if they are lighter skinned and have higher social and economic status than other Latinos. Racializing groups means that a group ordinarily seen as an ethnic group—that is, a group sharing a common culture and a common past—can become defined in racial terms, such as being defined as "brown people."

Some Asian Americans have also been racialized at various points throughout American history, defined, for example, as a "yellow peril." *Asian American* is a label, like *Latino*, that lumps together people who come from very different societies and cultures—indeed, societies that have at times even been at war with each other. Each group's history in the United States also differs, but the treatment of Chinese Americans, Japanese Americans, Filipinos, Korean Americans, and more recently, immigrants from Southeast Asia (Vietnam, Laos, Cambodia, and other places) has racialized some, though not all. Indeed, some Asian Americans may even be socially considered to be "White" while others are perceived in racial terms.

Seeing how groups can be "racialized" shows that race is not a fixed attribute of people and can change over time. In other words, just as race is socially constructed, it can also be "deconstructed." Some groups previously designated as "people of color" may even be "whitened" by gaining higher social and economic success. For example, European immigrant groups in the nineteenth and early twentieth centuries were sometimes initially defined as something other than white, but their ultimate success in America produced a perception of them as "White."

To sum up, race is created, changed, and potentially destroyed through the actions of human beings. This framework also helps you understand that the construction of race is now changing, especially as different groups now shape the American racial landscape. Sociologist Eduardo Bonilla-Silva has suggested that the United States could evolve into a *tripartite society*—that is, one that still divides people into black and white categories, but where there is a middle category he calls "honorary whites." Bonilla-Silva claims the tripartite system will include three general categories of people: *whites*, *honorary whites*, and the *collective black*.[6]

The white category includes non-Hispanic White people but also new White immigrants, totally assimilated White Latinos, and light-skinned multiracial people. "Honorary whites" would include light-skinned Latinos, such as Cubans and some segments of Mexican and Puerto Rican communities, plus various Asian American groups (Chinese Americans, Korean Americans, Japanese Americans), Filipinos, most multiracial people, and Middle Easterners. At the bottom of this stratified system will be the "collective black," including Black Americans; dark-skinned Latinos; Southeast Asian American groups, such as the Vietnamese, Cambodians, Laotians, and Hmong; recent West Indian and African immigrants; and reservation-bound Native Americans. According to this scheme, those on the nonwhite side of the color line are groups that share experience of oppression and exploitation.

At the core of this triracial system is white supremacy. In a tripartite racial system, groups in the category of white or honorary white are there based mainly on social class, but also on skin tone. While such a system, akin to that of parts of Latin America, appears to be race-neutral, it is nonetheless still anchored in the dominance of White people.

You can see evidence of this system of racial inequality emerging now. Many Asian Americans have equaled or surpassed White, non-Hispanic Americans in socioeconomic status. Some African American middle-class and elite people of color have been highly successful, in some cases surpassing working-class and poor Whites, who see themselves as increasingly left behind. Some Latinos, depending on their national origin and social class, already define themselves as White. Whether such a tripartite system will ultimately define the racial hierarchy in the United States remains to be seen, but the evidence we already see shows the fluidity of the concept of race and its connection to how people are treated in society.

If race is such a shifting and fluid idea—one that stratifies and ranks people—should we just abandon race altogether? The people of France did so in 2018 when the French National Assembly removed the word *race* from its statement protecting people from discrimination. The French constitution had guaranteed "Equality before the law for all citizens, without distinction of race, origin, or religion." The word *race* had been inserted in the Constitution in 1946 as a reaction against the racist theories and practices of the Nazi regime in Germany. The recent change was made based on the understanding articulated here that there are not distinct races in human populations and that to avoid racism, one must not classify people into racial groups.

People often will say, "I don't see race. I just see people as people." Although this may seem like a good-hearted expression—that is, one that refuses to categorize people into racial groups—the fact is that people "see" race all the time because of the meaning it has taken on in society. Even when people claim not to see race, race has major consequences, for example, in huge income and wealth disparities across different racial groups. Although the sentiment of "not seeing race" might be well meaning, it misses the point that race is real even though constructed through the doings of society.

RACE AND RACISM: A DOUBLE HELIX

A double helix is a shape formed by two curves wrapped around a central line. It is a good metaphor for understanding race, racism, and racial inequality. Think of racial inequality as the central line in the helix. Racism is the complex system of beliefs, ideas, and actions that surrounds this central fact—one of the "curves" in the helix. The second "curve" is the concept of race itself—made up to seemingly justify this system of human inequality.

This analogy turns the usual way people think about race upside down. Many people think of race as somehow reflecting meaningful differences between people—differences that are socially coded by "color." But when you understand that the meaning of race emerges from a system of racial inequality, then you understand that *racism produces race, not the other way around.* Without racial inequality, race would likely have no relevance other than showcasing the diversity of human life.

Perhaps it is normal to see some people, particularly those from outside your group, as "other." Throughout history people have been suspicious about others whom they perceive as somehow "different." But seeing outsiders as "others" is entirely different from establishing a social, economic, and political system in which some people are defined as innately inferior and then are treated as such. It is racism, not human difference itself, that creates such systems. Racism rests on the notion that race somehow distinguishes one human group from another. When that idea solidifies into a system of inequality, racism becomes the foundation for society's institutions. Although racism and ideas about race are found in the beliefs and attitudes of people in society, they are rooted in society's structures, not just individual minds—an idea explored further in the following chapter.

At the core of this book is the argument that racism is a complex system of beliefs and actions that overtly or covertly support an institutionalized system of racial inequality. Race and racism go hand in hand. Just as in the double helix, the intertwined strands of race and racism surround a core reality—a system of racial inequality. Once you understand this, you no longer think of race as an individual attribute. Rather, you understand that the idea of race has been created to support one of the most intransigent, inhumane, and yet enduring social systems: racial inequality.

Summing up what we have seen in this chapter:

- Race is a social construction.
- The concept of race is the false belief that one group of human beings is intrinsically different from and better than another.
- It is the treatment of groups, not individual attributes, that defines race and makes it meaningful in society.
- Racial inequality produces the idea of race, not the other way around.
- The meaning of race stems from the historical and contemporary treatment of groups.
- Race is contextual and its meaning changes over time.
- Race results from a collective and deeply social process that is intertwined with racial subordination.
- The meaning of race can be changed through human action.

Altogether, this means race is not just about individual identities and certainly not about biological makeup. Race is rooted in society, not individual character, and its meaning evolves as society changes. Race is somewhat like the shape-shifters popular in mythology, folklore, and children's literature. That is, race can turn into different forms, but it is still real. The idea of race is constructed in societies where there is a racial hierarchy—that is, where some presumably racial groups are valued more than others. Race may be fluid in how it is understood at different times, but it is still solid in that it is used to allegedly justify social hierarchies organized around presumed racial differences. Race is, in one sense, not "real," yet it is very real in its consequences. As the sociologist W. I. Thomas said long ago, "Situations defined as real are real in their consequences."[7] We cannot just make race go away without fundamentally changing the inequality on which it is based. Race may be constructed, but it nonetheless shapes people's thoughts about each other, the different outcomes of people's lives, and the everyday experiences of people of color, as well as of White people. Race then is richly layered in social processes of group behavior, individual identity, social and economic history, and the strong influence of society and culture.

CHAPTER 2

Feeling Race in Everyday Life

If you're tired of hearing about racism, just imagine living with it.

—Jon Stewart[1]

A FEW YEARS AGO, AN AFRICAN AMERICAN FRIEND OF MINE WAS sitting in a restaurant casually enjoying her dinner. Hanging across the back of her chair was a beautiful scarf I had knitted for her. As she was chatting with her dinner companion, she noticed movement behind her and quickly turned—only to see a White woman walking out of the restaurant with the hand-knit scarf in hand. "Hey, that's my scarf!" my friend said. You might think that the White woman would stop and mumble some apology, as if she had picked up my friend's scarf accidentally. But no: Much to my friend's surprise, the White woman emphatically insisted, "No, it's mine!"

Were the scarf a common off-the-shelf design, you might dismiss this as a simple mistake. It would be easy to confuse some scarves, but not this one. The scarf was hand-designed and hand-made, unique and beautiful. My friend confronted the woman who was stealing her scarf, but the woman continued to insist that the scarf was hers. Only when my friend reached out and took her scarf back did the women relent.

You might think this was just a simple misunderstanding—one that, luckily, did not escalate further. How would you feel had it been your scarf on the chair? If you are White, would you just brush it off, thinking it was some crazy or deranged person? Is it possible it was an innocent mistake? What kept the situation from escalating further? Should the police have been involved?

However you might interpret this situation, you cannot ignore that the scarf belonged to a Black woman and the woman who took it was White. Whatever motivated the White woman—greed, jealousy, desire, or mental illness—you can't ignore the role race played in this situation. For my friend, this was one more reminder of the everyday assaults racism inflicts on Black people and other people of color.

Suppose the woman stealing the scarf had been Latina or African American. Would the scenario have ended in the same way? What if the thief were a Black man? Just a slight variation on this already troubling scene and you can see the role race plays in everyday life. We often think about race in the "big picture," looking at such things as differences in economic status, segregated neighborhoods, and other large-scale issues in society. Those are surely important, but racism also operates in more up-close and personal ways.

IT'S THE LITTLE THINGS THAT COUNT

Outside the United States people do not understand how Americans see race. But see race we do—every day and in virtually every aspect of life. How we understand race depends, in part, on our own racial identity. But race is everywhere—in our daily interactions, in the cultural images around us and in the spaces we occupy.

White people might think race is only "present" when people of color are around or when the subject of race comes up in conversation. But even when White people think race doesn't matter, it does. When you sit in a meeting of all White people, race has shaped the fact that no person of color is present. When you live in a neighborhood where few, if any, people of color are present, race has shaped how and where you live. When you study history in school and that history is drawn mostly from European influences, race shapes what you learn—and what you have not learned. The list of examples is endless, including that White people do not have to think about race unless they choose to do so.

The invisibility of racism to dominant groups has been compared to the spikes in some parking lots. If you drive over them backward, they will shred your tires. Yet they are hardly noticeable as long as you go in the right direction.[2] Like the tire spikes, everyday racism can go unnoticed by White people who easily "flow" with the system. For people of color, there are constant reminders of one's status as "other."

Everyday racism refers to the common and repetitive behaviors that display racism on a regular basis. Such behaviors may be relatively mild instances, such as a slight, slur, or suspicious glance. At the extreme end, everyday racism may take form as a highly offensive comment, an aggressive act, even violence, such as when a white man, Patrick Wood Crusius, shot and killed twenty-two people with an AK-47 assault weapon at a Walmart in El Paso, Texas, after posting that there was a "Hispanic invasion" happening in Texas. As horrid as the crimes of white supremacy are, everyday racism is frequent and recurring. It is how racism is enacted in our daily life. In the aftermath of the El Paso massacre, many Latinas, for example, said they changed how they acted in public, fearful of speaking Spanish or going out alone and checking store exits whenever they were shopping. The impact of such fear has been likened to the fears Black people felt when lynch mobs terrorized Black people.[3] Everyday racism is demeaning and insulting at its least—extremely dangerous at its worst. By minimizing, ignoring, or threatening people of color, racism taxes people of color every day, even as it goes unnoticed by White people.

You can probably imagine or recall countless instances of everyday racism. Sadly, there is no shortage of examples. To note just a few that have made national news: A White woman accused an African American man who lived in her building of not belonging there, insisting quite emphatically that he show her proof of his residence. A US president calls a sitting senator from Massachusetts "Pocahontas." A White woman accosted a Latina mother in a Virginia restaurant because she was speaking Spanish. A White woman on a California highway made a slanted eye gesture toward a Korean American war veteran and yelled at him that this is "not your f-ing country; this is my country!"

You do not have to go to the national news to find examples of racism in everyday life, however. Troublesome encounters between White people and people of color are all too common, such as when a Latina student is criticized by her teacher for not speaking proper English or when a Black student is asked in class to "speak for her race." The examples are numerous and sadly familiar to those who experience them. They communicate that people of color do not belong, are somehow "other," and are not entitled to the same freedoms and rights as White people.

Some forms of everyday racism are verbal, some nonverbal, and some are direct behaviors, including potential violence. Verbal expressions of everyday racism include comments like the following: "Gee, you don't look Mexican—you look normal." And I cannot tell you how often I have heard women and people of color "talked over" in a meeting or witnessed a White person taking credit for an idea first suggested by a person of color. Even without a person of color in the room, everyday racism occurs, such as racist comments a White person might make in front of another White person. If the comments go unchallenged, racism lives on, unchecked.

Nonverbal examples of everyday racism include sometimes subtle behaviors, as when a White man steps away while talking with a Black man, when a White person assumes someone speaking with a Spanish accent must be an immigrant, or when someone thinks anyone wearing a hijab might be a terrorist. Even something as innocuous as the absence of decorative images of people of color in an office or school building can exemplify everyday racism. The absence of such symbols can signify that people of color and their cultures are somehow "lesser" or not as important as White culture. How would you feel if you never saw images of accomplished people who look like you in your workplace or school?

Psychologists use the term *aversive racism* to refer to the everyday actions, often unconscious, where White people just avoid interacting with people of color. These can be seemingly innocuous behaviors, such as the White woman who clutches her bag tightly as a Black man approaches or when someone avoids smiling at a Muslim woman wearing a hijab.

Everyday racism happens at the individual or "micro" level of society, but it originates within a broader power structure. Power is structured at the "macro" level of society—that is, in the history, institutions, and unequal relations between dominant and subordinate groups. Power is enforced through the large-scale actions of government and other social institutions but operates at the level of our daily experiences as well.

Acts of everyday racism are called *microaggressions*—those "brief and commonplace daily verbal, behavioral, or environmental indignities, whether intentional or unintentional, that communicate hostile, derogatory, or negative racial slights and insults toward people of color."[4] These can be momentary and subtle exchanges, possibly not even recognized by the offender, such as someone assuming that a Latina in a hotel is the maid or someone who addresses a Black professor in an elite club as one of the servers. People of color routinely experience these examples and more. A single incident of microaggression may seem small, but single instances add up.

In the overall context of racial inequality, the seemingly simplest things take on greater meaning. For example, everyone has probably experienced getting slow service in a restaurant, but people of color experience this on a routine basis. For people of color, any one instance of slow service can trigger a reminder of one's status in society. Further, if a person of color mentions a microaggression to a White person, all too often a White person will think—or even say—"It's not a big deal" or "You're wearing race on your sleeve," thus minimizing or negating the person of color's experience. The result for the person of color is yet another microaggression!

Researchers who have studied microaggressions conclude they are cumulative, becoming a constant burden for people of color. White people, on the other hand, tend not to see these intrusions on human dignity. Racial microaggressions are one of the consequences of living in a society structured by racial inequality. Even if you don't see it, race shapes everyday life.

THE COST OF EVERYDAY RACISM

Everyday racism means people of color must be on guard most of the time, especially when in the presence of White people. You may have to think about your every movement. Surely you need to be diligent about your public appearance. Most certainly you need to talk with your children, especially to young Black boys, about not talking back or acting surly if confronted by a police officer—a practice so common among African American parents that it is casually referred to as "the talk."

This is the racial tax people of color pay—not just an economic tax, but a psychic tax too. Surely, racism has an economic cost, but it has a social and cultural cost as well.

A simple true-false test illustrates these costs:[5]

Count the number of statements below to which you can respond "yes":

1. I can go shopping pretty well assured I will not be followed by security.
2. If my car breaks down on a deserted stretch of road and the police arrive, I can trust they will be courteous.
3. I have a wide variety of grooming products for people like me that I can buy in convenient places.
4. In school, my racial and ethnic heritage is presented in a thorough and affirming way.

5. If I have to go to the "person in charge" in a business or educational setting, I am likely to be facing a person of my race and ethnic background.

6. My coworkers always make me feel welcome.

7. I am rarely singled out because of my racial or ethnic identity.

8. I can trust employers to judge me based mostly on my skills and accomplishments.

9. If I get a good job or am admitted to a prestigious university, no one will think I got there because of my race.

10. If I look for housing, the agent will show me properties in mostly white neighborhoods.

11. In school, my teachers assume I am smart and capable.

12. If I try to hail a taxi when there are plenty available, a driver will likely pick me up.

13. I can look at mainstream media and see positive images of people who look like me.

14. If I shop in a convenience store, no one looks at me nervously.

15. If I want to buy a children's book for a relative or friend, I can easily find a variety of characters from my racial-ethnic background.

How many did you answer yes to? Chances are if you are Latino/Latina, Black, Asian, or Native American—anything other than White—you will have far fewer "yes" replies than will a White person. It is especially illuminating to take this quiz in a mixed-race group and compare everyone's total number of answers. This simple exercise can show the consequences of racism in everyday life—the subtle tax people of color pay—a psychic tax levied daily on people of color.

If they try, anyone can see the consequences of racism for people of color—but there is a cost to White people as well. That cost is certainly not anything near what it is for people of color, but it is there. The cost for Whites can be found in feelings of guilt, fear, or unease in the presence of people they perceive to be different from themselves. Racism also produces a lack of empathy among White people, perhaps making them feel the problem is insurmountable. Racism also results in the loss of cross-race relationships, stifling opportunities to learn from one another. Racism in school curricula means most people learn an incomplete and distorted view of our nation's history, culture, and the arts. At its worst, racism also produces fear—and, tragically—violence. Spiritual leaders have even concluded the cost of racism is so great that it creates a spiritual vacuum because it violates what they perceive as the essence of humanity—that is, caring for others.[6]

When we recognize everyday racism, we see racism as more than large-scale discrimination. Certainly, such things as income and wealth gaps, blocked opportunities, the educational gap, and other quantifiable forms of discrimination are significant. But the full force of racism operates even in the seemingly small things of everyday life. Racism penetrates our consciousness, conducts our daily interactions, and dehumanizes our souls.

Race, Space, and Place

Everyday racism also plays out in the spaces where we live. Do you live in a place with open space, nice views, good transportation, easily accessible shopping, and good schools nearby? Are the nearby homes and apartments well kept? Is your neighborhood safe? Who lives near you?

Chances are your answers to these questions reveal a strong degree of racial segregation. Racial inequality places us in racialized space. Sociologist George Lipsitz has written, "Relations between races are relations between places."[7] For most people in the United States this means that, despite some years of progress, we remain highly segregated from each other.

Racial segregation has been on the front line of the movement for civil rights, and with good reason. Some of the key victories of the Civil Rights Movement are landmark cases intended to reduce racial segregation, especially in housing and education. The Fair Housing Act of 1968 prohibits discrimination in housing. And the landmark 1954 Supreme Court case *Brown v. Board of Education* ruled school segregation unconstitutional. Yet now, more than half a century later, residential and educational segregation by race remain a stubborn reality of American life.

Chocolate Cities, Vanilla Suburbs

First coined by Reynolds Farley, the description of the nation's cities in flavorful terms depicts racial segregation well.[8] Many of the nation's largest cities are now "majority-minority," that is, most of their population is Black, Latino, and Asian while a large part of the White population lives in outer fringes and suburbs of the city. Certainly, cities in America have become quite racially and ethnically diverse and many White people, especially younger ones, are now moving back into cities, attracted by walkable neighborhoods, cultural resources, and some decline in the crime rate. But how integrated are cities, really?

This is a complex question. By some measures, residential segregation has declined across the nation since the 1960s, especially between Black and White Americans. But residential patterns have also become more complex, particularly given the influx of new immigrants and the increasing diversity of the population. Segregation patterns also vary significantly in different regions and between different groups.

It takes quite sophisticated quantitative analyses to calculate the degree of segregation (or, on its flip side, integration). How much racial segregation you see depends on where and how you look. Since 1990, racial segregation of urban neighborhoods has declined somewhat, but looking at whole metropolitan areas, segregation has increased significantly, especially between Black Americans and Whites. The suburbs have become more diverse, but Whites keep moving farther out of cities. Most metropolitan areas, such as Chicago, Detroit, and Milwaukee, continue to have very high degrees of racial segregation. The highest segregation in the United States is between Black and White populations. There is relatively low segregation between Asians and Whites, with Hispanics falling in the middle.[9]

The most common measure used is the *index of dissimilarity*—a measure of the distribution of groups in a given area. This figure measures how many people would have to move to reach an even distribution of groups in a given area. It can range from zero to one hundred. Analysts generally agree that an index of sixty or higher is indicative of a high degree of residential segregation.

This figure can be misleading, however. For example, if a given city is 70 percent Black and Latino and all its neighborhoods are 70 percent Black and Latino, then the index of dissimilarity would reveal no segregation because each neighborhood reflects the overall racial composition of the city. What if, however, most of the White population in this city lived outside the city limits—in its suburbs? Common sense would tell you this is a very segregated place. Social scientists use additional measures to assess the degree of *isolation* or *exposure* groups have to each other.

Measures of isolation and exposure find that in recent years segregation between Latinos and Whites and between Asians and Whites has actually *increased* even while the index of dissimilarity between these groups has been relatively constant. Also, the isolation of Blacks has declined rapidly in recent years, but only because of their greater exposure to other people of color. The exposure of Blacks to Whites has hardly changed in the past two decades.

Furthermore, in some places, segregation is so severe that social scientists now use the term *hypersegregation* to mean segregation occurring when nearly all the residents of a given area are of the same group. One-third of all Black metropolitan residents now live in hypersegregated neighborhoods. It is telling, however, that we do not think of neighborhoods that are almost all White as hypersegregated, but they are.

Perhaps segregation would not matter so much if the neighborhoods of so many people of color were not also poor. Hypersegregated neighborhoods—at least those populated by people of color—are typically characterized by concentrated poverty. *Concentrated poverty* occurs where 40 percent or more of the population in a given area lives below the federal poverty line. Black Americans and Latinos are those most likely to be living in such neighborhoods. Further, even when they earn five times more than low-income White families, Black families are more likely to live in neighborhoods marked by poverty. This means if you are Black, even if you are not poor, you are more likely to live surrounded by poverty.

George Lipsitz provides a telling summary of the impact of racial segregation. He writes that relegating people to different spaces in society produces unequal access to education, employment, transportation, and housing—and exposes communities of color disproportionately to environmental hazards. At the same time, he says, Whites enjoy "privileged access to economic opportunities, social amenities, and valuable personal networks."[10]

The consequences of racial segregation are many and can include such basic things as having access to healthy food. It is well documented that there are fewer supermarkets in low-income, racially segregated neighborhoods. Communities of color often live in what have come to be known as "food deserts." Small neighborhood stores where food is more expensive are more common in such places. Racial minorities are twice as likely to have fast food chains in their neighborhoods, food sources known to be linked to poorer health. Low-income, minority neighborhoods are also dotted with payday lenders, pawn shops, and other places that charge exorbitant fees, leaving people with the fewest resources actually paying more for what they need.[11]

Feelings of personal safety are also affected by the spatial patterns of racial inequality. A recent Gallup survey found that over three-quarters of White Americans feel safe walking alone at night in the area where they live, compared to only two-thirds of Black Americans. Not surprisingly, men in every group feel much safer than do women. Class matters too, but even at low income levels, people of color feel less safe than Whites in similar income brackets.[12]

Racial segregation lessens social interaction among racial-ethnic groups. In integrated neighborhoods, there is typically block-by-block segregation. Even in somewhat well-integrated neighborhoods, Black, Latino, and White neighbors rarely visit each other's homes, do things together, or share personal details about their lives.[13]

If these consequences were not enough, the dominant society heaps negative judgments on people who live in predominantly Black or Latino neighborhoods, especially if the residents are poor, regardless of the people's actual character, values, and ideals. Racial segregation is particularly hard on children. Racial minority families with children are actually even more segregated than families without children.[14]

Indeed, the impact of racial segregation is hard to underestimate. At the individual level, people separated from each other are less likely to develop friendships or know each other well enough to refute racial stereotypes. For people of color, the disadvantages that come from residential inequality can mean more disruption in their lives. Eviction, for example, disproportionately affects African Americans and, to a lesser extent, Latinos. Frequent moving also disrupts children's education, exacerbating the already existing inequities in education along racial lines.

Sociologist Eli Anderson identifies what he calls *white space*—that is, the perception that people of color have of places where they are "typically absent, not expected, or marginalized when present."[15] When people of color enter a white space, they likely feel uncomfortable, as if the place is "off limits." White people, on the other hand, rarely perceive the same thing, instead imagining white space to be neutral or unremarkable.

White space underscores that racial segregation and integration are not simply about numbers. *Segregation and integration are fundamentally social constructs* that involve not just who is present and who is not, but also how people relate to and perceive one another. In a society marked by racial segregation, the vacuum in interracial contact gives more force to the cultural stereotypes that are pervasive in everyday life.

CULTURAL RACISM: IT'S IN THE AIR

You might not expect, for example, that when you run your errands and go to the grocery store, you would be confronted with an array of racial and ethnic stereotypes. But the next time you go to a grocery store, walk through every aisle and make note of the images of people you see on various products. Here is what you might find:

Pancake mix has a smiling image of a modern Aunt Jemima, lighter skinned than in the past but an image that still is based on a racial stereotype. Are you looking for drink mix? Margarita mix has a stereotyped Latina on its label—long, flowing hair, big red lips, and an alluring smile. A beguiling Native American woman is there to offer you butter. American Indian chiefs in full headdress and feathers adorn corn meal labels. If you want some salsa, Paul Newman's likeness beckons, dressed as a stereotypical Mexican bandit complete with a mustache and a sombrero. If food labels are any indication, Asian Americans don't even exist. White men don't get off easily either: Check out the paper towels with big, brawny, muscular men looking like they have spent their lives working out in the gym.

A few products apply different racial-ethnic group images on different versions of the same thing: Black women's faces appear on some hair coloring products, but the very same product provides a white version too. Deodorant is also packaged with different racial-ethnic images on the exact same product. Does this mean your hair and underarms are the only places where diversity is allowed?

If you are looking for racial integration, you will have to look hard because the only place in the store where you will see racial-ethnic groups together is in the cereal and diaper aisles. Is the message that it is safe for children of different racial-ethnic groups to be together, but not adults?

You may never have paid particular attention to these and other everyday images, but they are pervasive and influential. Racial and ethnic images are packaged and sold through a variety of products, media forms, and other avenues where social stereotypes are produced and consumed. You might think they have no impact on you or anyone else, but research shows otherwise.

The representation of race and ethnicity in popular culture and the media is massively important in shaping our views of each other and ourselves. What significance do these cultural images have? How did they originate and how have they changed? How do people understand them and at times challenge them?

The images and messages of racism are so pervasive in society that educational expert Beverly Tatum says they are like "smog in the air."[16] Some people may not even be aware of such images—unless, of course, you are highly offended by them or develop a more critical eye. Even when they are not obvious, racial imagery constructs an understanding that lingers in the imagination. Such images produce *cultural racism*, meaning the implicit and explicit messages that "affirm the assumed superiority of Whites and the assumed inferiority of people of color."[17]

Chiquita Banana is an example. First introduced in the 1940s, Chiquita Banana was an advertising symbol that promoted the nutritious value of bananas. Chiquita Banana was represented by a stereotypical Central American woman, who appeared initially as recently coming off a boat from "near the equator." The actual figure was a banana, but the banana was designed as a hip-swirling woman who appealed to men with her flirtatious winking and suggestive dancing. At the time the image was introduced, the men, women, and children who worked on US-owned banana plantations in

Central America were being subjected to grueling work conditions and serious illness from pesticide poisoning. Wildly popular, the mocking image of Chiquita Banana became especially notorious in the 1940s when Brazilian actor/singer Carmen Miranda became a Hollywood star. She was widely known for her elaborate and garish style, one that was highly commercialized within the United States, including the image of her with a large bowl of fruit on her head. The Chiquita Banana image still advertises bananas. Few now question this demeaning image of a Latina, dressed in presumably Latin clothing (which few Latinas actually wear) with fruit on her head. You can even purchase this look in such common places as Pinterest and Halloween costume stores.

Images like Chiquita Banana are manufactured. They create an illusion that sells products, markets entertainment, and teaches us what to think. Cultural racism buttresses a system of white supremacy by trivializing, ignoring, and/or ridiculing people of color. This is why racial stereotypes, such as a White person appearing in blackface or someone posing as a person of color at Halloween, are offensive to so many. Enacting such stereotypes, even when claiming it is only for fun, makes people of color the vehicle through which White people demonstrate their dominance: They can playact being a person of color without paying the cost of being mistreated because of race. In the end, cultural racism deeply influences our self-concepts, our understandings of each other, and our knowledge and information about race in society.

STEREOTYPES AS CONTROLLING IMAGES

Especially if you have no other way to know a racial or ethnic group different from your own, the images in popular culture have a profound and lasting impact on how you think about race. The cartoons you watch as a child, the music you listen to as a teen, the video games you play, the television and film characters you love, the books you read, even the news you watch—all these forms of culture shape your perception of others and yourself.

You cannot help but be influenced by stereotypes in these cultural outlets.

Stereotypes in popular culture are so powerful that they have been called *controlling images*. A concept coined by scholar Patricia Hill Collins,[18] controlling images are part of a system of racial domination. Stronger than the term *stereotype*, a controlling image restricts and manipulates how people think, thus serving the interests of the most powerful in society. Why otherwise are Latinos typically cast in stereotypical roles: as laborers, as hypersexual, or as criminals? Whose interests are served by having Native Americans, such as Chief Wahoo of the Cleveland Indians,* used as sports mascots and depicted as warlike and cartoonish at the same time? It is difficult to overestimate the power controlling images have to shape racial ideas and beliefs. They view people of color through a narrow lens that diminishes, distorts, and misrepresents reality.

Controlling images also create *racial frames*—that is, fictitious scripts that produce narratives about how we see ourselves and others through the lens of race. Racial framing refers to "the racial perceptions, stereotypes, images, ideologies, narratives, and emotive reactions used to make sense of a given situation, experience, or issue involving racial matters."[19] For the most part, the dominant racial frame, whether inadvertent or not, projects white supremacy—that is, that White people are superior, everyone else, inferior. Three themes, in particular, stand out in racial frames—or narratives—about people of color, namely criminalization, "otherness," and sexualization.

Criminalization

The media vastly overrepresent people of color as criminals. This is not a new narrative, because cultural images have historically targeted Black men as criminal threats. The expansion of local news

---

* After years of protest and criticism, in 2018 the Major League Baseball commissioner and the owner of the Cleveland Indians removed the image of Chief Wahoo from the Cleveland Indians' uniforms. The logo was removed from the stadium, although merchandise featuring the logo continues to be sold.

coverage over the years has, however, added to this representation. Local news affiliates need to fill the time allotted to them and do so inexpensively. Images of violence (fires, shootings, and the like) provide more vivid images than would otherwise come from non-violent crimes such as tax evasion, embezzlement, or government kickbacks. The result has been a dramatic increase in media images of urban crime where people of color tend to be concentrated.

Recently, immigrants from Mexico and Central America have been viciously targeted by the criminal narrative—even though immigrants commit far fewer crimes than either native-born people or second- and third-generation immigrants.[20] Even the president of the United States, Donald Trump, has stoked fears about so-called caravans of immigrants, as if hordes of gang members were coming to America to rape and murder law-abiding citizens. The criminalization frame plays on age-old fears about immigrants as "invaders," especially when they are perceived as "brown"—that is, racialized. This racial frame became deadly when Patrick Wood Crusius posted such a claim on a social media website before going on a shooting rampage in El Paso.

Criminalization of immigrants is all too familiar. During the early twentieth century, Chinese and Japanese immigrants were routinely portrayed in popular advertisements as a "contagion," "pollutant," and "peril," clearly implying that Asian immigrants threatened the fabric of American life—White American life, that is. These images were used to generate public support for the eventual exclusion of Chinese and Japanese immigrants, just as the criminalization refrain is being used now to build public support for more punitive immigration policies.

Making People "Other"

Another common narrative is that of people of color as "alien" or "other." Such imagery has been common in the nation's past, as just about every immigrant group has at one time or another been labeled an alien invader. In the 1850s Catholic immigrants were seen as Papists who threatened American liberties. Chinese laborers were seen as a "yellow peril." Southern and Eastern European immigrants in the nineteenth century were defined as criminals and madmen who threatened American values. Just about every group except English Protestants has, at one time or another, been perceived as invading the nation. The alien narrative is especially pointed now, reflected in language such as "illegal aliens." Ask yourself, what different connotation is there in calling someone an "illegal alien" versus an "undocumented worker?" The first usage focuses on unlawfulness, reinforcing the criminalization narrative. The second emphasizes the labor that immigrants provide—a far more positive image, even though it still invokes the image of illegality.

The alien narrative depicts people as somehow "other," emphasizing their foreignness and presumed difference from imaginary "real Americans." When human beings are described as animalistic, cheaters, and undeserving, they are dehumanized—a precondition for racism. Superstar athlete Serena Williams, for example, has been frequently referred to in animalistic terms—highly racist depictions. Narratives of otherness also thwart any chance of developing empathy toward groups perceived as different from oneself.

Sexualizing People of Color

Controlling images of people of color also routinely oversexualize people of color. African American men are portrayed in a potent mix of sex and violence. Black, Latina, and Asian women are sexualized in particular ways, too. African American women athletes, such as the successful Williams sisters in tennis, are routinely described in terms that emphasize their sexuality, such as constant commentary on Serena Williams's curves. Music videos, for example, showcase Black women with big butts and large breasts. Latinas are portrayed as "hot," seductive, overly emotional, and dressed in loud colors. Muslim women are stereotyped as erotic and shrouded in veils, not that different from how American

Indian women are sexually depicted. Asian American women are routinely sexualized as well, as "dragon ladies"—exotic, sensual and mysterious, but domineering. Asian men, on the other hand, are stereotyped as asexual, passive, and "geeky." In each case, the bodies of people of color become places where racism is scripted, especially for women. Like the alien narrative, sexualization dehumanizes and distorts people of color, even while presenting them for the enjoyment and voyeurism of White people and other onlookers.

Controlling images are how everyday racism permeates our lives. People of color are, of course, not the only groups so distorted. Controlling images misrepresent many groups, including women, people with disabilities, lesbian, gay, bisexual, and transgender people, and older people. Although all groups can be distorted through the media, people of color get distorted in particular ways with serious consequences for their health and well-being.

It Gets to You: Racism and Health

Given the pervasiveness of racism in daily life, it is not surprising that there are significant disparities in health along racial lines. The psychic costs of everyday racism are huge, but there are physical costs as well. Studies have found, for example, that when Black people interact with White people, their stress levels increase. Interestingly, a similar pattern occurs for White people: When interacting with Black people, White people's heart rate increases.[21] Clearly, we would all be better off if we could stop, or at least reduce, everyday racism.

Everybody knows what stress is. Whether working long hours, studying for exams, or just feeling frazzled by too much to do—everyone feels stress at one time or another. You probably have even experienced *white coat syndrome*—the elevation in blood pressure that commonly occurs just by a visit to the doctor's office. Such an elevation in blood pressure, though, is typically fleeting.

Chronic stress, though, can produce hypertension. Hypertension is a physiological fact, but physicians know that blood pressure varies depending on social and environmental conditions. It is, in fact, telling that it is hard to find a Black man in America who does not have high blood pressure. Researchers consistently find that African American men, as well as American-born Latinos, have a higher prevalence of stress than do White Americans. Hypertension based on racial inequality can be life-threatening. Constantly being on the alert for racial insults or other microaggressions wears people down. Simply put, cumulative exposure to racism is detrimental to one's health.

On virtually every measure, racial-ethnic minorities in the United States have poorer health than do White people. Furthermore, health disparities for people of color have persisted over time and at all levels of income and education.[22]

You can see this by answering a simple question: Did you get a good night's sleep last night? Being short on sleep is correlated with an increased risk of early mortality, and how well you sleep is strongly associated with your racial, ethnic, gender, and occupational status. If you are Black, you are more likely to be short on sleep than Whites and Latinos. Among Blacks and Latinos, being short on sleep increases with higher professional status, perhaps contrary to what you might expect. For Whites, the reverse is true—Whites are shorter on sleep when in lower-status work roles. Black women professional workers have the least sleep of all and, maybe this will surprise you, but professional White women are the least likely to be short on sleep.[23] Surprising as they may be, these facts point to the physical toll of everyday racism.

How long you are likely to live is also a matter of your race and ethnic status. Life expectancy—the average number of years people born in a particular year can expect to live—has increased for all groups in the United States over time, but significant differences remain based on race (and on gender). Women in every racial-ethnic group live longer than their male counterparts, but African American men have the shortest life expectancy of all.

Hispanics in the United States actually have a longer life expectancy than do White non-Hispanics—a phenomenon referred to as the *Hispanic paradox*. You would think that Hispanic life expectancy would be comparable to that of African Americans, given similarities in their socioeconomic status. Experts do not yet understand this paradox, although one likely reason is the lower rate of smoking among Hispanics.

Infant mortality is also shockingly high among people of color. Infant mortality is measured as the number of infant deaths in a given year per 1,000 births, counting those under one year of age. Overall, infant mortality is quite low in the United States, compared to other nations, but infant mortality among African Americans and Native Americans gives a more disturbing picture of the nation's health. Rates of infant mortality for these two groups are comparable to those in some of the poorest nations in the world—largely because of the high rates of poverty among Black and Native Americans.

Environmental racism also disproportionately exposes people of color to environmental wastes and other hazards, as the nation clearly witnessed during the lead poisoning of the Flint, Michigan, water system. Throughout the United States, toxic waste facilities and other pollutants are more likely to be located in the neighborhoods of people of color. The National Association for the Advancement of Colored People (NAACP) has found, for example, that a huge proportion of African Americans (80 percent) live within thirty miles of a coal-powered plant, a fact that may explain the much higher rates of asthma found among African American children.

Not only are areas populated by people of color most likely to have toxic waste facilities nearby, but there is less enforcement of environmental regulations in areas populated by people of color. At the same time, however, people of color have taken an active role in organizing movements against environmental racism.

Researchers who study environmental risks have concluded that exposure to toxic substances is "a pathway through which racial inequality literally gets into the body."[24] Is this because polluters deliberately discriminate against people of color and poor people? Does class explain toxic waste dumping more than race? Or is dumping just a matter of market forces because it is cheaper for companies to situate landfills, toxic waste dumps, and other pollutants in less economically valuable neighborhoods?

Of course, there is a class dimension to environmental pollution. Toxic waste is also found in poor and working-class White neighborhoods. Class alone, though, is not a sufficient explanation. Both race and class are significant in explaining patterns of pollution, and race has effects of its own.

CREATING A CULTURE OF AFFIRMATION

Everyday racism can feel overwhelming, but there are ways to challenge it. One way to do so is to create counternarratives that undermine the power of controlling images and that confront the microaggressions of everyday racism. But how?

The first step is to be aware of the many forms everyday racism takes both in social interactions and in the images of popular culture. Second, especially if you are in the dominant group, understanding how it feels is a path to empathy. Beyond empathy, you have to be willing to make changes, including possibly changing your own mind about things you have taken to be true. None of this is easy and it does not happen quickly.

Although popular culture produces and reflects everyday racism, it can also be used to subvert it. Hip-hop artists know this and have used their talents to challenge dominant constructions of racism. Performance artists have also dramatized new images and identities that undermine dominant narratives. In fact, throughout history, people have organized to resist racist images and to insist on more affirming images of diverse people.

Creating and supporting positive representations of people of color would create a *culture of affirmation*. Standing up against everyday racism is culturally affirming, as is resisting the demeaning, but rampant, images of people of color in popular culture. Here are some ways you, regardless of your racial identity, might do this:

- If you hear someone make a racist comment, ask the person how they would feel if such a comment were made about them or their group.
- Expose yourself to the viewpoints of different racial and ethnic groups, including in the media.
- If you see racial stereotypes in the media or other forms of popular culture, contact the person or group in charge and tell them you find such images offensive.
- Never minimize reports from people of color about the racism they experience.
- Have a small group take the quiz on the racial tax and then discuss how racism appears in everyday ways. Have each person identify one thing they could do to intervene to disrupt everyday racism.
- Educate yourself about racial health disparities and support organizations and people who are working to reduce them.
- Join an organization that is part of the environmental justice movement.
- In general, use a critical eye when observing interaction with people of color and when viewing popular culture; ask yourself if people of color are being treated with the respect and dignity they deserve.

A culture of affirmation can transform our understanding of race and ethnicity and be part of the movements toward racial justice. This does not mean White people should appropriate the culture of people of color—as when privileged groups consume and "claim" the culture of an oppressed or colonized group. Actor Amandla

Stenberg, who is herself African American with Danish and Inuit roots, describes this tendency well: "What would America be like if it loved Black people as much as it loves Black culture?"[25]

Racial boundaries, hierarchies, and definitions are challenged by those who produce new visions for what is possible. All people can work to produce more affirming views of people of color, but the burden of doing so cannot fall solely on people of color. Because race is socially constructed, it can be changed. Building a culture of affirmation is one way to do so. At the same time, we need to get smart about how our attitudes reproduce racism, even though—as we will see in the next chapter—attitudes are only one part of challenging racism.

CHAPTER 3

Who, Me?

I'm Not a Racist, But...

Whites can express resentment toward minorities, criticize their morality, values, and work ethic, and even claim to be victims of "reverse racism." This is . . . racism without racists.
—EDUARDO BONILLA-SILVA[1]

WHEN WAS THE LAST TIME YOU HAD A CONVERSATION WITH someone about race? What did you hear? What did you say? Your answers very likely depend on your own racial identity—and who you were talking to. If you are a person of color, you likely talk about race with other people of color regularly, probably less often with White people. As a person of color, talking about race probably invokes a whole host of emotions: When talking with White people, you might feel guarded, fearful, or even angry, depending on the context and the other person's demeanor. When talking with other people of color, you might feel more relaxed because of a sense of shared understanding. Of course, among good friends— including with White friends—people of color can usually be more candid and trusting. All these feelings come from the reality of racism, which leaves people of color on guard and feeling vulnerable in many situations.

On the other hand, if you are White, you probably feel a different range of emotions when talking about race. To begin with,

White people in American society have the luxury of not having to talk or think about race every day, as do people of color. Most often, White people are afraid to talk about race—especially in the presence of people of color. After all, no one wants to be called a racist. Even well-intended White people who see themselves as free of racial prejudice are typically afraid they might say something "wrong" or offensive. Instead, they simply say nothing.

When White people do talk about race, they often do so with an air of confidence, maybe even downright arrogance, as if they know all there is to know about people of color. It's often surprising how reassuringly White people make assertive statements about race—even when they have studied little about the nation's race relations and may not even know any person of color in a close or meaningful way. Listening to White people talk about race, you might hear, "I don't see race; people are just people," or "I don't have anything against Black people; I just don't think there should be government handouts to people who are not willing to work hard"; "I know someone who was denied a job because it had to be filled with a minority person"; or "Some of my best friends are people of color; I'm not a racist."

You might have even heard someone say that people of color can be racist too—if they make generalized and negative statements about White people. "Reverse racism" is the phrase commonly heard, as if racism is simply a matter of negative judgments about other people—that is, prejudice. But, as you will see, racism is more than prejudiced attitudes. A White person can even be opposed to racism and yet benefit from a system of racial inequality. This is because racism is built into society and it is more than individual attitudes.

People tend to think of racism as a matter of prejudiced ideas—that is, attitudes that target particular groups in demeaning and negative ways. We are all familiar with examples of prejudice. Calling Mexican immigrants "criminals and rapists"; referring to immigrants as "infesting" our country or "stealing our jobs"; or referencing Muslims as terrorists: These are clear examples of prejudice.

Such overtly prejudiced remarks are repugnant to many people, even though they are more commonplace than we might want to believe. No doubt about it, openly racist remarks and the people who state them are a threat to civil society, but they are not the only form of racism, as we will see.

Overt racism is easy to spot. We saw it in the slaughter of people in El Paso because the killer thought Hispanics were invading Texas. We saw it as anti-Semitism during the 2017 Charlottesville white supremacist march when neo-Nazi supporters chanted, "Blood and soil" (an old slogan asserting Nazi superiority) and "Jews will not replace us." You have likely heard it in allegations about Black people and supposed welfare dependence. You heard it when the president said four women of color in the US Congress should "go back to where they came from." Overt prejudice of any kind is usually obvious and deeply disturbing, but prejudice and racism are not the same thing. Although they are often used interchangeably, prejudice is an individual attitude, whereas racism is built into the structure of society. Racism can be reflected in individual attitudes, but it is also present even when prejudiced attitudes are not expressed. You can understand this if you just ask yourself, "If we eliminated racial prejudice, would racism just go away?" The answer is no.

PREJUDICE AND POWER

Social scientists have a long history of studying prejudice and its consequences, most notably beginning with social psychologist Theodor Adorno. The son of a German Jewish father and Italian Catholic mother, Adorno left Germany in the 1930s, fleeing persecution by the Nazis. After first going to Britain and then to the United States, he returned to Germany after the end of World War II. Adorno was fascinated by how the human mind could allow people to commit atrocities, such as the mass extermination of Jewish people during the Holocaust. His answer: prejudice.

Adorno thought prejudice originated in feelings of insecurity and a perceived threat from others. He is best known for identifying a particular personality type, labeled the *authoritarian personality*. People with authoritarian personalities typically have little tolerance for difference, are rigid in their judgments about others, and are highly obedient to authority. Adorno concluded that people with an authoritarian personality are especially prone to prejudice.

Adorno's work was followed by social psychologist Gordon Allport, who wrote a classic book, *The Nature of Prejudice*, published in 1954. To this day Allport's concept of prejudice guides how prejudice is studied and understood. Allport proposed that prejudice emerges in particular social and historical contexts. Those contexts shape how people see each other. Allport helped us understand prejudice is not just the result of certain personality types. Instead, it emerges when there is inequality between different groups. He defined prejudice as a hostile attitude toward people simply because they belong to a particular group, as if members of the group are all alike and share some objectionable characteristic.

Prejudgment is central to the concept of prejudice.* A prejudiced person judges people based on presumed characteristics, often knowing little else about them. Prejudice may be directed against any group of people—women, LGBTQ people, old people, Muslims, Catholics, Hindus, Jews, even fat people, heavily tattooed people, maybe even bald people. This shows how common prejudice is and that it is not always racial. The different groups prejudice targets are distressingly numerous. When it comes to racial prejudice, prejudice is generally negative, such as in seeing certain racial groups as culturally deficient, prone to crime, or lazy. Prejudice can, though, be a positive judgment, such as in thinking all Asians are smart or all Native Americans are spiritual. Even seemingly positive expressions of prejudice might, however, insult someone because of the generalization on which prejudice rests.

---

* Prejudice is a noun and should be used accordingly. People often misuse the word, using its adjectival form (prejudiced) when the noun (prejudice) is appropriate. To illustrate: a person may have a *prejudiced* attitude but exhibits *prejudice*.

Prejudice is widespread in many societies and contexts. It stems from *ethnocentrism*—the belief that one's group is superior to all others. Perhaps ethnocentrism is unavoidable, because people tend to see others through the eyes of their own group experience. But when ethnocentrism becomes tinged with race (or sex or religion or any other lower-status characteristic), prejudice develops and can become deadly.

Prejudice is about perception—that is, how people see other people. Perception, not reality, forms prejudiced attitudes. Prejudice is also learned. It does not just "come naturally." It might be learned in the family, but it is also learned in peer groups and through the many cultural stereotypes rampant in society—especially in the mass media, as we saw in the previous chapter. However, because prejudice is learned, it can be "unlearned." That is, education and learning about diverse groups is a powerful antidote to prejudice.

No one is free of prejudice, but certain facts predict the likelihood of someone being prejudiced or not. People with more education are far less likely to be prejudiced than people with less education, although, admittedly, educated people may simply be more practiced in knowing how to suppress prejudiced thoughts. Generally speaking, older people are more likely than younger people to express prejudice. People with fundamentalist religious beliefs tend to be more prejudiced than others, particularly if their religious beliefs promote a restricted or closed-minded view of the world. At the same time, it is important to remember religious faith has also been a major historical impetus for social justice movements, such as in mobilizing the Civil Rights Movement. In other words, prejudice emerges in a social context. It is not surprising then that prejudice is more common in some groups than in others.[2]

Prejudice relies on stereotypes—oversimplified caricatures about the members of a social group. Stereotypes flourish particularly when people have little information about other people. They typify or categorize people who are presumed to be part of a group.

Perhaps it is inevitable for people to categorize others. When you meet someone for the first time, you instantaneously categorize the person, first on race and gender, perhaps also by age and social class. Stereotypes can be positive, or even neutral, such as the stereotype that all Norwegians are blond. But it is negative stereotypes that are so harmful, especially when they target less powerful groups, such as team mascots that stereotype Native Americans.

In the United States, over the course of history, virtually every racial and ethnic minority group has been subject to denigrating and insulting stereotypes. The Irish have been stereotyped as hotheaded drunks, Italians as Mafia members, Polish Americans as stupid, Mexican Americans as violent and hypersexual. Name a group and you can probably instantly imagine some of the stereotypes that have been negatively associated with that group.

Prejudice, however, is not just some vague or abstract feeling. Prejudice emerges in the context of power relationships. This is why stereotypes about people of color are so offensive. Think about Halloween costumes. If someone dresses up like an Italian gangster, most people are not offended, although such a costume does stereotype Italians. But if a White person dresses up like a Black pimp or gangster, Black people are highly offended. Likewise, when White people dress in blackface or White women pretend to be Latina maids (or, worse, prostitutes), people are deeply offended. Why? The answer lies in the power relationships that are part of the system of racial inequality. There is simply not an equal playing field in this society when it comes to race. Consequently, ridiculing a racial or ethnic group packs extra insults that would not be a problem were there equivalencies in how people are perceived and treated in society. There are not.

THE HARM OF STEREOTYPES

Stereotypes have far-reaching consequences, even though many think they are harmless. An Asian student who is only average in math skills may feel extra pressure to do well because of the stereotype that all Asians excel in math. A blond woman who is very smart may have to be extra careful not to appear dumb because of the stereotypes about blonds. Maybe she will just joke about it, as if to distance herself from the stereotype. African Americans may need to be especially neat in public to avoid negative judgments. Latinas, stereotyped as hypersexual, may need to appear demure or shy to avoid the risk of a harmful characterization. For people of color, avoiding any suggestion of a stereotype adds to the stress of everyday life. Perhaps someone will even overplay a stereotype as a way of resisting it. However they appear, stereotypes have serious consequences for people's self-confidence, academic performance, and even physical health.

Social psychologist Claude Steele and his colleagues have demonstrated how attuned people are to the stereotypes about them. *Stereotype threat* happens when people feel the risk of confirming, through their own behavior, stereotypes others have about them.

Here is how Steele and his colleagues discovered this: Black and White research subjects were told in a series of laboratory experiments they were about to take a test that was "a genuine test of their verbal abilities and limitations." Other research subjects, matched by race with the first group, were told they should try hard, but the test would not evaluate their actual ability. Only in the first scenario, when a stereotype was present as part of the test instructions, did Black and White test scores actually differ—and significantly so. In other words, Black test takers, when aware of the stereotype of them as less smart than White students, actually perform less well when the stereotype is invoked. Without the threat of the stereotype, Black and White test takers perform equally well.[3]

This result has been repeated in numerous other experiments. Each time the results are the same: Feeling stereotype threat actually lowers African American student performance. Furthermore, this finding has been shown to occur for other groups, such as when women are aware of the stereotype that they are not good at math or when Mexican American students (immigrant or not) are faced with the stereotype that Mexican immigrants have little command of English. With the presence of stereotype threat, people's performance suffers.

Aside from laboratory experiments, you can imagine other scenarios where stereotype threat produces apprehension and then inhibits a person's behavior. Imagine a Latina whose professor makes a comment in class stereotyping Latinas. Wouldn't her performance in class be negatively affected? Turning the tables, when students hold stereotypes about Asian or Latino faculty members that the faculty member does not speak English clearly, might the mere presence of this stereotype influence how well a faculty member teaches? If a hospital patient makes a slur against a Muslim or Asian nurse, might the nurse not do the job as well? In that case, both parties are hurt—the patient and the nurse! Even seemingly innocuous comments, made through no particular ill will, can invoke stereotypes that affect the behaviors of people who are keenly aware of the stereotypes about their group. In the end, stereotypes harm us all.

ARE WE ALL RACIALLY BIASED?

Social scientists have produced volumes of research on how prejudice and stereotypes affect social behavior. The results show that people may not even be aware of the prejudices they hold about different groups, but their beliefs still guide their behavior. Something as subtle as how closely you stand to someone or whether you look someone in the eye can reflect prejudice.

The influence of unconscious bias has been demonstrated through something known as the *Implicit Association Test*. The test, done by individuals on a computer, shows images of different people who are identifiable by their race. As the images move rapidly by, the test taker quickly associates the image with either a positive or negative second image. Bias is shown by the frequency with which people associate people of color with negative characteristics and White people with positive characteristics.

Time and time again, this cleverly designed experiment reveals the implicit biases most people hold. Just beneath the surface of our conscious thinking lie judgments and associations that are triggered even when we might not realize they are present. Numerous studies now document the implicit biases people hold against various groups. Implicit bias is how culture leaves an invisible imprint on our minds.

By becoming aware of these unconscious associations, we can work to overcome them. The practical implications are many. For example, social psychologists are now utilizing implicit bias tests to help police officers in some cities recognize the implicit biases they hold, surmising that with training they will not so quickly associate Black men with criminality—a deadly association.[4]

RACE AND RESENTMENT

Prejudice has had a strong and lingering presence in the United States. Yet its overt expression has declined, at least to some degree, since the era of Jim Crow segregation. The rise of overtly expressed racial prejudice in recent years has, however, shocked many people and exposed a deep, underlying vein of racial hatred in American society. Racial attitudes are, at times, vitriolic while at other times—or among different populations—they are more subtle.

Now, for example, so few people express overt prejudice that survey researchers no longer ask the questions earlier used to measure racial prejudice. For example, in 1942, a full two-thirds of White Americans said they favored racially segregated schools, compared with only 7 percent who said so by 1985. Researchers no longer ask this question. If they did, it is likely few respondents would say they favor segregated education—even though schools remain just as racially segregated as they were in the 1980s.[5]

Not surprisingly, Black Americans, Hispanics, and White Americans strongly disagree about the nation's racial progress. Only 27 percent of Black Americans say race relations now are good; the vast majority (71 percent) think race relations are generally bad. On the other hand, close to half of Whites (44 percent) think race relations are good; 56 percent of Whites say they are bad. Black Americans and Hispanics (50 percent) are also far more likely than Whites (41 percent) to think race relations are getting worse.[6]

Public opinion polls are also revealing growing racial resentment among White people. Racial resentment is reflected in beliefs that people of color are somehow "getting something for nothing" or "getting special benefits just because of their race." Racial resentment also includes the idea that White people, not people of color, are the aggrieved group; substantial numbers of White Americans believe this.[7]

Social scientists have shown feelings of racial resentment to be closely linked to various behaviors and attitudes about social issues. People expressing high rates of racial resentment were more likely to vote for Donald Trump in the 2016 presidential election, and they are more likely to support punitive criminal justice policies. Racial resentment is also strongly linked to White attitudes about immigration, such as in thinking immigrants are a drain on the economy, that we should make it harder for immigrants to enter the country, and that White Americans are losing economic ground because of immigrants.

At its core, racial resentment stems from perceiving the well-being of White people as threatened by the supposed success of people of color. Oddly enough, racial resentment is surfacing even while White people continue to have higher incomes, more wealth, and lower unemployment than people of color.[8] The belief that Whites are losing ground is just not true, but the strength of this belief shows how powerful racial attitudes are in driving social and political behavior. Perception, even when contrary to reality, is a potent force, especially when linked to strongly held feelings about one's own social position in the world.

NOT A RACIST BONE IN MY BODY:
RACISM WITHOUT RACISTS[9]

No one wants to be called a racist. Accusing someone of racism may spark anger and, very likely, a defensive response. Picture a racist and who do you see? Someone waving a Confederate flag? A White working-class man shouting racial slurs, perhaps while marching with white supremacists? Someone hanging out at a party with friends and making a racist joke? Most people find such attitudes deplorable, but racism is more than individual attitudes. Racism is also not the same thing as racial prejudice, even though prejudice is one manifestation of racism.

Racism can be covert, and it might be unintentional. Racism is not always obvious, and it occurs in many forms, not all of which involve individual attitudes. Racism can be subtle, unless you are on the receiving end of it. To fully understand racism—its causes and its consequences—you have to look to society, not just to individual attitudes, beliefs, or behaviors.

To see society's influence, think about the connection between prejudice and discrimination. Does prejudice cause racial discrimination? Most people think so, but step back and think about this connection. Prejudice is an attitude. Racial discrimination is behavior when people are treated differently based on their race. Bigots are people whose prejudiced attitudes very likely lead to racial discrimination. But there can be situations where someone might be quite prejudiced but doesn't discriminate. An example would be a bigoted police officer who would not discriminate for fear of penalty or a bigoted employer who might dislike Asians and Latinos but will hire them because the company rewards bosses who employ a diverse workforce. In both cases, prejudice exists but discrimination does not. In other words, attitudes and actions do not always line up.

There can also be situations where people neither express nor feel prejudice and, yet, their behaviors result in racial inequality.

An example would be parents who send their children to mostly White private schools so their children can get the best education possible. They may genuinely not be prejudiced, but discrimination occurs nonetheless when racial minority children do not get the same opportunity. Racial disparities appear even in the absence of explicit prejudice or bad racial attitudes. In other words, people may be free of prejudice and not discriminate based on race, but racial inequality persists.

These different examples show that prejudice does not by itself cause or explain racial inequality. Certainly, attitudes matter and changing them is a necessary step toward racial justice, but reducing prejudice alone is not sufficient for reducing inequality by race. Moreover, when you stop thinking about racism as based in attitudes (that is, prejudice) and instead think of racism as based in society (not just in individual minds), your view of racism changes. Racism exists in the very structure of society.

Racism can be manifested in people's thoughts and actions, but it is more complex and more systemic than individual attitudes or acts of meanness. Racism is a system of power that subordinates people who have been defined as a "race," as we saw in the first chapter of this book. Racism isn't merely the action of bad people, and it need not be motivated by irrational or prejudiced thoughts. Racism may not even be apparent to those who benefit from it. Fundamentally, racism is systemic in society—an entire constellation of ideas and behaviors that benefit one group at the expense of another.

In fact, racism has structured the very institutions comprising US society. Although evidence of racial inequality is vast, most people fail to see its systemic nature. More likely, someone will say, "I don't see color" or "Race doesn't matter; we are all alike." But racism shapes everything in our society. It structures our interactions with other people and how we perceive ourselves.

Some will say there is "reverse racism" or "people of color can be racist too." But this cannot be true once you understand racism as a system of power, advantage, and disadvantage. People of color can be prejudiced, but they do not hold racial power in a racially unequal society. In that sense, they can't be racist. Restricting awareness of racism to individual bigotry misses the societal basis of racism—that is, institutional racism.

Institutional Racism

Racism emerges because of relationships of domination and subordination between groups socially defined as "races." This means racism is about exploitation, not just about people's beliefs. Racial beliefs buttress a system of racial inequality, but if we ignore how race is constructed because of specific social and historical events, we miss that institutions have produced and sustain racial inequality.

It took Black activists in the 1960s to tell social scientists that racism was more than prejudiced attitudes. The radical activist Stokely Carmichael (Kwame Ture) and political scientist Charles Hamilton described racism as both overt and covert and as taking two entangled forms: individual racism and institutional racism. Individual racism is what we have seen as bigotry and prejudice. Institutional racism, by comparison, is less overt, but as Carmichael and Hamilton assert, it is "no less destructive of human life." In their words,

> When white terrorists bomb a black church and kill five black children, that is an act of individual racism, widely deplored by most segments of the society. But when in that same city—Birmingham, Alabama—five hundred black babies die each year because of the lack of proper food, shelter and medical facilities, and thousands more are destroyed and maimed physically, emotionally and intellectually because of conditions of poverty and discrimination in the black community, that is a function of institutional racism.[10]

Carmichael and Hamilton's work changed how we think about racism. Institutional racism is a system of power and inequality. It can certainly be manifested in people's thoughts and actions, but it is a system of racialized power—or what sociologist Joe Feagin calls *systemic racism*.[11] Within such a system, White people benefit because racial advantage and disadvantage accrue to people independent of individual thoughts and beliefs. Of course, not all White people benefit equally, but no White person experiences the racism that is common among people of color. Saying that racism is deeply embedded in the institutions of society means racism is a social structure—one resting on certain beliefs, but as a *system* of racial inequality and racial power. Changing individual attitudes is not enough to dislodge this embedded system of inequality.

Some people will say racism equals prejudice plus power. That is, however, too simple a formulation. Racism is not just the summation of many attitudes with power thrown in. It is a principle of social domination that has been the very foundation for social institutions in the United States. Ever since slavery and the first writing of the Constitution that defined a slave as three-fifths of a person, race was used to exploit Black labor and buttress white-dominated social institutions. Slave owners could even believe they "cared for" their slaves, while denying them basic human rights. Racism, even when paternalistic, rationalized an economic system that robbed Black people of citizenship, property, and personhood while granting certain White people total economic and social power. This makes white privilege central to any discussion of racism.

Now, even with slavery long gone, the manifestations of this cruel system of human exploitation remain with us—as do the many racial injustices that have been perpetrated since slavery ended. Although most people may not directly witness actions that deny people of color human rights, the legacy of the past continues to shape racial inequality today. We will explore this more in chapter 5 of this book, but, for now, the point is that racial inequality has been built into national institutions, even while the efforts of people of color in building those institutions (through slavery, labor in various industries, private care in people's homes, and other contributions) have been ignored.

White Supremacy and White Nationalism

When you live in a racially unequal society, being White carries various benefits that might not even be visible to those who have them. In the words of author Peggy McIntosh, whiteness is like an "invisible knapsack."[12] Various tools in the knapsack give White people resources others simply do not have.

Those resources might be a social network of well-placed friends who can provide access to jobs or internships. The many advantages of being White can be as ordinary as not being followed when shopping in your local market or department store—that is, the privilege of not being "suspect." Even the freedom of being able to drink to excess or pass out drunk in college is an example of white privilege (possibly class privilege, as well). On college campuses, for example, Black and Latino students drink far less than White students, most likely because they fear the racism they will have to endure if they are seen as "out of control."

In a society structured by racial inequality even everyday actions have different racial consequences. I once had students do experiments to demonstrate this. In one experiment, two students—one Black, the other White—tried to pay for a sizable purchase in a department store using only coins. As one conducted the transaction, the other carefully observed the clerk's reaction to this odd behavior. When the White student paid, the clerk's reaction was astonishment, but with laughter and a good-natured exchange. The Black student, on the other hand, was peppered with questions and treated with hostility. The clerk became very angry, not wanting to take the money at all. Two students, same behavior—but a different outcome only because of race.

In a similar experiment, two students (one White and one Latina) borrowed a baby and a stroller. Each student separately pushed the stroller through the local mall while carrying a very large number of packages. First, the White student dropped all the bags while the Latina recorded people's reactions. Then the Latina student did the very same thing, dropping all the bags, while the White student observed. In the case of the White "mother," several people quickly rushed to her aid. The Latina "mother" was completely ignored.

These experiments, which you could try yourself, show some of the everyday ways white privilege is bestowed, even when it might not be noticed by many people. In a system of racial inequality, whiteness is the assumed "normal" way of being; everyone else is defined as "other." This is also reflected in the underrepresentation of people of color in the media. When present, people of color stand out; they seem like "exceptions." Many will even overestimate their presence. An Asian American doctor, for example, will be referred to as "the Asian doctor." A White doctor is just a doctor.

White privilege makes White people seem to be presumed to be "deserving," while people of color are seen as taking advantage because of their race. We've all known someone who is perpetually loud, but White people can be loud without it being attributed to their race. White people can also act very righteous about their attitudes about race, even when they are woefully uninformed.

Of course, not all White people experience these advantages in the same way. Tell a White working-class man he has "white privilege" and he is likely to laugh in your face—that is, if he is being kind and doesn't launch into a tirade. In some ways, he is correct because his class disadvantage relative to wealthy Black men is obvious. White working-class men and women may be less well-off than the Black or Latino middle class, but they will never have to worry someone will think they got a job "because of their race." Clearly, class matters along with race, but race also shapes people's life chances independently of class.

In a system based on white supremacy, people will believe (even without thinking about it) Whites are more virtuous than others, such as by holding a strong work ethic. This is true even while people of color have to work harder to get to the same place. Children learn this early, ascribing certain characteristics to different racial groups at a very young age. A team of Harvard psychologists has shown that, more than just recognizing race, as early as age three, very young children have learned to associate Black, Asian, and Latino faces with anger; White faces, with happiness.[13]

White privilege also shows up in the fact that White people do not feel compelled to speak out about race, as people of color must do on a regular basis. White people also don't like to think they are privileged because of race. They can deny that race matters, congratulate themselves on being anti-racist, or even stay silent about racism when they see it—all while reaping racial privilege simply by being white.

As described by writer and educator Robin Diangelo, *white fragility* is the unease White people feel when they are challenged to see their connection to a system of racism.[14] White people quickly become defensive when challenged to acknowledge racism. They are likely to think other people, not they, are responsible for racial inequities. Consequently, you might hear, "Slavery was bad, but I didn't have anything to do with it. Don't hold me responsible!" When confronted with the reality of racism, White people tend to deny, argue, withdraw, or simply remain silent. Although not deliberately intended as such, this is how White people protect and sustain white privilege.

Few White people imagine themselves as supporting or benefiting from white supremacy, but white supremacy is the underlying pattern supporting racial inequality. White supremacist beliefs fall along a continuum, though. Sometimes they are subtle, other times, horrifically visible. At its ugliest, white supremacy appears in the form of white nationalism. *White nationalism* is a series of beliefs linking white dominance with national identity. Like other forms of nationalism, white nationalism is based on feelings of white superiority, often accompanied by a perceived sense of threat from some presumed "racial other."

What drives this egregious form of racism that has once again become apparent? Sociologist Mitch Berbrier has identified several parts to white nationalist beliefs, including perceiving oneself as a victim of racial discrimination; claiming white rights are being abrogated as people of color have increased rights; feeling stigmatized and shamed by people of color; sensing one's white identity is under assault; and believing there is a threat to the survival of White people. Each of these ideas is heightened as people of color become a greater proportion of the population.[15] These perceptions help explain the current resurgence of white nationalism, a phenomenon that has caught many by surprise and terrorized communities of color.

Especially when organized as a social movement, White nationalism is extremely dangerous, although as we have tragically seen, it is potentially lethal through the actions of single individuals, such as those who burn or desecrate Black churches, Islamic mosques, Sikh temples, or Jewish synagogues and cemeteries. Extreme forms of white supremacy should not, however, distract us from its more subtle forms. As long as White people are perceived, overtly or covertly, as somehow more deserving, harder working, and more entitled, then white supremacy persists. In other words, outright racial bigots are not the only racists in America. Racism may not look like it has in the past or as it appears in white nationalism, but its presence remains.

THE MANY FORMS OF RACISM

Now that the racial and ethnic population of the United States is more diverse than ever, the old "Black/White" division that defined Jim Crow is largely a thing of the past. Overt barriers to the advancement of people of color have been somewhat lowered. There is greater acceptance of mixed-race relationships. There are visible people of color in positions of power in America. These changes have led many to think we are "beyond race" and that whatever racial inequities still exist must be the result of something else. With these changes, though, have come new forms of racism. Racism is a dynamic social system that changes as society changes. It can even take different forms in the same period of time.

Color-blind racism is the idea that it is best to just ignore race and look at people as if they are all alike. In other words, if people would only overlook race and not see "color" or "difference," then the effects of racism would just vanish. Color-blind racism is a form of denial—denial that racism exists even while society remains organized around racial inequality. Someone might say, "I don't see race; people are all alike."

You can see the fallacy in color-blind racism—and the reason it so offends people of color—through this analogy: If you are a woman, how would you feel if someone said to you, "Gee, I never think of you as a woman"? Or, if you are a man, would you be insulted if someone said, "Gee, I never think of you as a man"? This is precisely what happens when people of color hear color-blind racism.

People who express color-blind racism often congratulate themselves on being open-minded, well-meaning people. Likely, they are. But although color-blind racism appears not to be about race, it is actually all about race. No one appears to be outwardly racist, and yet racism continues. This is what Eduardo Bonilla-Silva means by "racism without racists."[16]

Color-blind racism can slip easily into blaming people of color for their own predicament. If racial inequality is not about race, what do people think it is about? Class? Culture? The attitudes of people of color? By ignoring race and placing the cause of racism on those most harmed by it, color-blind racism shifts responsibility for racial inequality away from those who have the most power to do something about it.

Related to color-blind racism is *laissez-faire racism*, meaning "hands-off" racism.[17] Laissez-faire racism includes the idea that anti-racist policies are no longer needed to address racial inequality. It might be reflected in statements such as, "I shouldn't have to pay for someone who is not willing to get a job," or "We spend too much time focusing on race."

Laissez-faire racism often assumes individual effort pays off and that those who fail have not tried hard enough. It ignores the obstacles people of color do, in fact, face and it ignores that most of the highly successful people in the United States have had some advantage or assistance to get where they are, whatever their racial background.

I'll use my own experience to illustrate. I grew up in a modestly middle-class family, one that experienced some degree of upward class mobility through the generations. My grandparents were working class; my parents, not educated beyond high school. My parents always stressed the importance of education. Because I initially attended very good public schools and because I had the support of very good teachers, I loved school and worked hard to succeed at it. I was in school at a time when the government, both state and federal, invested a lot in public education, spurred in part by the space race with the Soviet Union.

Later, when I went to college as a first-generation student, I earned a full scholarship to a prestigious private Southern university that paid my tuition and expenses. When, during my first year, I encountered a sexist math instructor and, as a result, did very poorly in my honors calculus class, I lost my scholarship, had to leave the very expensive college, and enrolled in a public urban university. I worked full-time to pay my way, but tuition was cheap: I remember it being about $125 per quarter.

I went to graduate school after a supportive faculty member said to me, "You're good at this (then, sociology and research). You should go to graduate school." My immediate response was, "What's that?" When I learned I could apply for a teaching assistantship that would pay a living stipend (though a small one) and cover my tuition, I quit my secretarial job and went to graduate school. I borrowed some money from a state-funded student loan program with a very low interest rate and that I did not have to repay until one year after I completed my final degree. I emerged from graduate school with a PhD in hand, only $3,000 in student loan debt, and a job offer.

There is no question I worked hard, but I had support from several state and federal programs helping me along the way. First, the government had a strong investment in high-quality public education. Second, state and federal programs made it possible for me to attend college and graduate school without the burden of a huge amount of debt. Third, I was hired as a faculty member as part of a strong commitment to affirmative action—in my case, based on gender. I was qualified for the job and was never accused of getting it "because of my race," but affirmative action was a definite benefit to me at a time when the "old boys' network" was breaking down because of affirmative action policy. Finally, as a White woman, I never had to experience racism. In fact, I did not even think much about racism until awakened by the social movements of the 1960s and by my education as a sociologist.

Imagine how different such an experience would be for a person of color now who wants to succeed but does not have the support I had *and* who also has to deal with racism, and possibly sexism, too. Of course I worked hard, but hard work and individual effort do not, by themselves, predict success. Yet laissez-faire racism asserts we need not intervene to promote success and that racism will somehow fade away on its own.

Laissez-faire racism and color-blind racism are powerful belief systems because they rest on the national value of individualism and the tenet that all people are created equal. But as my experience and those of many others show, even with individual effort and the cultural belief in individualism and equality, racial inequality can—and does—shape the opportunities people have available to them.

Denying that race matters is to be blind to the realities of racial inequality. Saying it is about something else erases the significance of race in society and in the experiences of people of color. When White people deny what people of color know, they deflect attention from one of our most serious national problems. Even a glance at contemporary events—the resurgence of white nationalism; racist behaviors on college campuses; police shootings of Black people; persistent poverty among Latinos, Native people, and African Americans; the educational achievement gap; and more—indicates race still matters.

BEYOND INDIVIDUAL BELIEF

If there is one thing to be learned from this chapter, it is that eliminating racism is not simply a matter of identifying individuals who hold racist views and then changing their minds. Nor is it a matter of reeducating people away from prejudice, although doing so is one important step in an anti-racist agenda. As long as race continues to shape all matters of human life—interpersonal relationships; individual and collective identities; social and economic opportunities; mental and physical health; education; and criminal justice—challenging racism must confront the institutional patterns that structure the system of racial advantage and disadvantage. This means we need to develop practices and policies to challenge and transform institutional, not just individual, racism.

Racial inequality is complex, shifting, and stubborn. Beliefs about race and racism are, likewise, complex and shifting. When such beliefs focus only on individual attitudes, they divert attention from the institutional basis of racial inequality. In the following chapter, we will look more closely at some of the beliefs that continue to thwart actions to reduce racial inequality.

CHAPTER 4

What Did You Say?

Contesting Commonsense Racism

I believe that the systemic racism we still see in this country toward people of color is terrifying, sickening, and prevalent.
—TAYLOR SWIFT[1]

THE BASIC CONTOURS OF RACIAL INEQUALITY ARE FAMILIAR TO most people, at least in a general way. People know many people of color are poor. They hear there are various disparities in some of life's most basic facts: health care, education, housing, and work. They might have witnessed injustice for people of color at the hands of the criminal justice system. This is not the place to review or debate these realities, but a few basic facts are:

- The income gap between Black and White households is the same as it was in 1970—Black families still earn only about 60 percent of what White families earn. For Hispanics, the gap is 72 percent, also unchanged since Hispanics were first enumerated in the US Census in 1970.
- On virtually every measure of health (life expectancy, infant mortality, health insurance coverage, and so on), African Americans, Native Americans, and Asian Americans have poorer health than White Americans. Paradoxically, Latinos have better health.

- In schools, Latino and Black students are now more isolated from White students than was true in 1980. The poor quality of "majority minority" schools means there is a large racial gap in educational achievement.
- Housing segregation between White and Black Americans has declined somewhat in recent decades, but Latinos and Asians have become more residentially isolated from Whites.
- African American men are six times more likely to be imprisoned than are White men; Hispanic men, twice as likely.[2]

Unless they are blind to documented facts, people know these things are true, at least in a general way. These issues are not, however, problems only for people of color. Income inequality, health disparities, low educational achievement, poor housing, and incarceration affect White people too. Actually, White people are a numerical majority of the poor—an often-overlooked fact. White people, like others, are also deeply concerned about health care, especially the cost and availability of health insurance. White families, just like other families, also want a good education for their children. Affordable housing is also a growing concern for all people, especially in our nation's cities. And it is possible that a White person might confront injustice at the hands of the police or the court system.

It is not that people of color are the only ones to experience these problems. Anyone might confront injustice in society. These various social problems are traumatic for anyone who experiences them, but people of color are far more likely to experience such problems than are most Whites. Further, when problems arise, they tend to cascade, particularly for people with limited resources. We also have to keep in mind that not all people of color are oppressed by poverty, nor are all beset by social problems. Yet as long as racial disparities exist, society as a whole is imperiled because inequality breeds social conflict. Explaining the persistence of racial disparities is a critical step in developing social policies to address it, but we need to get past some of the misconceptions that are common in explanations of racial inequality.

IT'S ONLY COMMON SENSE . . . OR IS IT?

Ask someone, especially a White person, why they think the Black crime rate is as high as it is and you will likely hear, "It starts with the family." Or, someone trying to explain the economic status of people of color might say, "It's not about race anymore. It's about class." And in one of the most common reactions that surfaces, you might hear, "It's their cultural values. They just don't try hard enough."

You hear these explanations in public conversations, on talk radio, in social media, and among friends. They are what I call *commonsense racism*. Ordinarily, we think of common sense as a reasonable, yet ordinary, way of understanding something. Someone might say, "Use your common sense!" But common sense, even when widely believed, can be very misleading. That is surely the case with commonsense racism.

Commonsense racism is a narrative—that is, a story. Like other stories, commonsense racism takes many forms and engages different themes, but fundamentally it is just that—a story. Like other stories, commonsense racism is fiction, but it is believable because it relates to things people *think* are true—not because commonsense racism *is* actually true. The narratives of commonsense racism resonate because they tap into underlying American values, especially those of individualism and personal achievement. Commonsense explanations of racism then appear to be legitimate, but in the end, they only reproduce racial inequality.

The different forms of commonsense racism are what scholar Joe Feagin calls *white racial frames*.[3] White racial frames embed various stereotypes, prejudices, assumptions, images, and emotions that together purport to explain racial inequality. They are widely shared myths—that is, stories—about why racial inequality persists. They circulate within the public, as people—especially White people—make claims about why racial inequity persists.

As Feagin points out, these narratives reinforce white supremacy. How so? They either indirectly or directly position White people as somehow superior—harder working, with stronger families, more culturally sophisticated, and so on. Often stated with great certainty and with claims to good intentions, these narratives are pernicious because they do not question the racial status quo. Rather, they defend it—either inadvertently or intentionally. Because they are presented as "common sense," they reassure their narrators that society is basically sound and that racism would somehow disappear if only people of color (and especially poor people of color) would change their values, work harder, and conform to the dominant culture. Commonsense racism conveys a particular understanding of racism—even though an incorrect one. These everyday explanations of racial inequality have an incredibly strong grip on people's understanding of racial inequality.

Whether you call these common explanations of racial inequality racial frames, stories, narratives, or commonsense racism, they all have something in common: They are uninformed by the extensive scholarship documenting the actual causes and consequences of racism. In other words, they ignore the systemic nature of racism in society. Instead, they blame people of color for their own predicament and deflect attention to race onto something else—usually social class or people's misguided values. Below are some of the repeated refrains in commonsense racism.

REFRAINS OF RACISM

The Color of Fear is a documentary film in which eight men—two African American, two Latino, two Asian American, and two White—meet at a retreat to discuss the state of race relations in the United States. Their discussion brilliantly captures the frustration and fury people of color feel when White people say or do things that are clueless about the workings of racism. Emotionally raw and deeply insightful, the film (directed by Lee Mun Wah) chronicles the men's discussion. They share their thoughts and feelings about racism, including anger, hurt, and sorrow, but also demonstrate a willingness to question and challenge each other.

Throughout the film, the men of color talk about their experiences with racism. At one point in the film, as the others nod knowingly, one of the Asian men describes the hurt he has felt by being the only person of color in all-White classrooms. The Black, Latino, and Asian men also relate their fears of traveling in rural, mostly White areas. They point out that part of being White means having the privilege of never having to admit your experience is different from that of people of color. As they talk, one of the White men—David—seems oblivious to what the men of color are telling him, even while they try to explain how tiring it is to have to constantly educate White people about racism. But David doesn't seem to understand and keeps insisting, "We are all just alike—Americans," and then he says, "If only people of color would stop blocking their progress by letting their attitudes about Whites limit them, then we would all be better off." At one point, David accuses Victor, a Black man, of "always going in the wrong direction," proposing that Victor should instead "look for something within himself to make him feel equal, instead of blaming Whites."

The Asian American facilitator interrupts and then asks David, "But what if what the men of color are saying is true?" David responds, "Well, that would be awful because you don't want to think that the world is that harsh. It is very saddening to me because I don't want to believe that man can be so cruel to himself or his own kind."

This is the moment in the film where the men find connection. Victor responds to David, "Well, now I can work with you."

Among other things, this film captures some of the misunderstandings many White people have about race. I've often heard Whites say, "If these young Black women would just not have babies," or "Why can't they just get a job?" or "It's about family breakdown," and countless other examples of what I am calling commonsense racism.

Perhaps you've heard such statements yourself. Maybe you agree with some of these ideas. Or maybe when you've heard such claims, you thought they were not quite right, but didn't know how to respond. When I hear such claims, I usually wince and wish I had the perfect retort—a kind but gently prodding response that unpacks the assumptions embedded in each. Let's examine some of these common beliefs.

"It's Just in Their Culture"

There is a long-standing refrain of blaming the victim in discussions about race in America. Certain phrases come to mind: "a tangle of pathology," "poor family values," "too lazy to work," or "playing the race card." These and other caricatures tell people of color, especially if they are poor, that there is something wrong with them and that if they would just change their attitudes or values, their lives would be better. If only it were that easy!

Sometimes blaming the victim is subtle, such as when a person says, "It's a cultural thing" or "If they would just try harder." Other times, the idea is more overt, such as from former Congressman Paul Ryan who, while trying to explain economic conditions in America, said: "We have got this tailspin of culture, in our inner cities in particular, of men not working and just generations of men not even thinking about working or learning the value and the culture of work, and so there is a real culture problem here that has to be dealt with."[4]

Following Ryan's comments, critics argued his words "inner city" were a veiled reference to race. You certainly hear such victim-blaming claims directed against various people and groups, but they are most common against people of color—especially, but not exclusively, if they are poor. The White poor do not fare so well up against victim blaming either, but blaming the victim is especially toxic when mixed with racial—and also gender—stereotypes.

Black women, for example, are harshly judged as "welfare cheats"—allegedly having more children to increase their welfare checks or using food stamps to purchase frivolous items. Given the shrinkage of the safety net since federal welfare law changed in 1996, such accusations would almost be laughable were they not so hurtful. Nested in these stereotypes is the suggestion that people are getting something for nothing and are just making bad choices—about work, about families, and about their lives more generally.

Facts about current welfare policy debunk such notions, as does understanding the societal conditions people of color—and the poor, especially—face. Federal welfare policy (Temporary Assistance for Needy Families, or TANF) requires recipients to work and there are limits on how long you can receive TANF support. There is a two-year limit on any given incidence of support and a total lifetime limit of five years for TANF support. This makes a so-called cycle of dependency impossible.

States vary in the particulars of how they implement welfare laws, but in no state do TANF payments lift a family above the federal poverty line ($20,231 in 2018 for a family of three, including two children). The median payment for a family receiving TANF is a meager $447 per month. Families receiving food stamps get on average only $145 per month.[5] Many states also place caps on welfare payments so a mother who has another child cannot receive additional assistance if she was receiving help before her pregnancy. Put simply, the purchasing power of TANF benefits is now well below the level it was in 1996, when current welfare legislation was passed.

The Supplemental Nutrition Assistance Program (SNAP), commonly known as food stamps, is similarly surrounded by myths. Federal law stipulates that unless you are pregnant or mentally or physically disabled, you cannot receive food stamps for more than three months in a given three-year period unless you are working or in a job training program. In 2019 the average food stamp benefit for a family of three was $379 for a month; divided by three, that comes to $128 per person for a month. Assuming three meals per day, the benefit computes to $1.42 per meal for each of three people. To think people are getting something for nothing, even if they occasionally buy a small treat for themselves or their child, lacks any empathy for those trying to support their children on such meager funding.[6]

Despite these facts, the refrain is always the same: "If only they would ____." Fill in the blank: work harder, not have so many children, get married, stay off drugs—you name it. The very title of federal welfare policy—The Personal Responsibility and Work Reconciliation Act—suggests that the best social safety net is for people to just take care of themselves.[7]

Moreover, claims about the so-called culture of poverty have been widely debunked. Well over fifty years of sound social science research tell us that values and attitudes don't explain poverty, yet commonsense racism continues to blame people for their own plight. How unyielding racial stereotypes can be!

Unlike the belief that poor women of color do not value marriage, careful research finds that they do. They just don't think it is attainable for them.[8] Given the high rates of joblessness and imprisonment among young men of color, these poor and young women of color are likely correct. Further, in a culture that glamorizes motherhood and defines women's identity as primarily family-focused, it is little wonder young women of color seek motherhood to affirm a positive identity, as do many young White women. Especially when you are devalued by the dominant culture, it is not surprising that someone would seek an affirming identity.

To be sure, some people, including people of color, make bad decisions—often very bad ones that can slide them into poverty or aggravate an already difficult life. An early pregnancy, dropping out of school, using drugs—these are all behaviors that can spin you into a downward spiral. But the very problems so often attributed to the poor choices of people of color are also common in

White, middle-class, and well-to-do families where family problems are more easily hidden from public view.

Despite stereotypes to the contrary, most people of color do not experience grinding poverty, substance abuse, or crime. Truth be told, large numbers of people of color actively resist such behaviors and work hard to counter the dynamics of racism. People of color and the White poor are, however, more often subjected to public scrutiny by formal institutions (such as the police, social service organizations, and school administrators), making them more vulnerable to social disparagement. In comparison, when White people make bad, possibly life-changing decisions, their failure may be interpreted as a personal flaw, but it is never seen as representative of their race.

People make choices within a context. In the United States, that context is widely believed to be fair and unbiased. White people, especially, do not perceive racial discrimination as readily as do people of color. In one public opinion poll, when asked whether inferior jobs, income, and housing of Black Americans is about "mostly discrimination" or "mostly something else," the vast majority of White people (83 percent) say it is about "something else." Although "something else" is not defined in the poll, one can't help but suspect "something else" is a reference to deficient cultural values.

In fairness, a large number (60 percent) of Black Americans also say racial inequities are about "something else," so it is difficult to interpret exactly what this poll reveals. But when asked more specifically whether Black Americans have as good a chance as Whites to get any job for which they are qualified, to get a good education, or to get any housing they can afford, Black and White people strongly disagree about whether there are equal opportunities. Two-thirds of Whites say Black Americans have equal job opportunities, compared to only 30 percent of Black Americans. Seventy-two percent of Whites and only 40 percent of Black Americans think Black Americans have equal housing opportunities.[9]

Perhaps it is just easier for people to blame individuals for their own failure than to acknowledge the social roots of racial inequality. I am pretty sure most people do not intend to be mean when they attribute racism to people's values. Quite the contrary, when I hear commonsense racism, I think people are generally well meaning and are trying to be understanding. On the other hand, I also hear White people stating their beliefs with great earnestness and self-assuredness, even when they have very limited information about or contact with people of color. I have also heard some White people rail on about the alleged problems with people of color with such conviction that they have vicious looks in their eyes as they speak.

Victim blaming depicts people of color as somehow *other*, and not fully *American*—a racial frame now falling especially hard on Mexican and Central American immigrants. Defining someone—either a person or a group—as "other" is the first step toward dehumanization—an essential ingredient of racism. When large numbers of people think cultural deficiencies and individual attitudes are the basis for racial inequality—or any form of class inequality, for that matter—such beliefs generate hostility and result in stingy social policies.

One of the ironies of blaming cultural attitudes for racial inequality is that most people of color—as well as immigrants—hold very strong beliefs in core American values, including personal drive, the value of education, and a desire for individual success. Somehow in the context of blaming the victim, this fact gets overlooked.

For sure, cultural attitudes cannot be completely dismissed. All human beings develop cultural practices and attitudes as they adapt to the conditions of their lives. This is the very definition of human culture. Cultural values are not just free-floating ideas existing independently of their context. When that context robs you of your human dignity, your best response might be the creation of alternative, perhaps resistant, cultural attitudes. Society produces different outcomes for different groups, so you should expect people's cultural attitudes and values will not necessarily be the same. To the extent that some cultural values and attitudes might differ, they are likely the result, not the cause, of unequal conditions.

"It's Not Really about Race; It's about Class"

People are often reluctant to attribute the causes of racial inequality to race per se. Instead, they will say social class is the primary problem of racial inequality. Certainly, well-off people of color can be seen most days—as media anchors and commentators, in positions of national power, as heads of major companies, and in other high-status places. At the same time, local news media routinely broadcast images of violent crime in poor communities of color, making poverty among people of color very visible, even if in stereotyped and misleading ways. The juxtaposition of the success of many African American, Native American, Asian, and Latino individuals with widely broadcast images of poverty makes it plausible for people to think race is now surpassed by class in determining people's life chances.

In truth, there are disturbingly high rates of poverty among Black Americans, Latinos, Native Americans, and some Asian American groups. Poverty within every racial-ethnic group also exceeds that of White Americans, including among Asians. The likelihood of growing up poor if you are Black or Latino is nearly three times that of White children. Social class definitely matters in producing the economic status of people of color, just as it does for everyone else. But does class override the influence of race?

If you were to tell an African American investment banker who gets stopped by the police in an affluent neighborhood that his experience is about class and not race, he might laugh in your face. When someone mistakes a Latina professor on a college campus for the building custodian, is the insult about class or race? As we have seen, most people of color live with the everyday eruption of racism—*regardless of their social class.*

There are, no doubt, class differences within communities of color, and there has been a strong middle class among people of color for many years. Because the Civil Rights Movement opened new doors for many, better-off people of color were well positioned to benefit from these opportunities. As a result, the Black and Latino middle class expanded and has become more visible. But class alone does not explain this development. It took specific race-based policies, such as civil rights legislation and affirmative action, to expand the Black and Latino middle class. Class and race have also intertwined in different ways at different historical times.[10]

Under slavery, race operated as a caste system—a form of racial apartheid. Race stood apart from class in determining your standing in such a race-based society. Slavery was a class system explicitly based on racial power. Racist state policies also continued under Jim Crow segregation where race, more than class, defined one's place in the social order. Until relatively recently, race almost completely superseded class in proscribing the position of Black Americans in society. Still, although strict racial segregation is now a thing of the past, it would be wrong to think that race no longer matters.

With the expansion of an industrial economy in the early twentieth century, the connection between race and class shifted. Manufacturing, not agriculture, became the economic driver. As Black workers moved into the North and Midwest during the Great Migration to find industrial work, they competed with White workers for jobs. Racial conflict then crosscut with class conflict. Class conflict between workers and owners was intense, with owners stoking racial and ethnic conflict to try to divide the working class. At the same time, White workers often tried to neutralize Black competition by excluding them from labor unions.

Race and class conflict played out in various industries and cities during this volatile period. In the West and Southwest, miners organized for better working conditions. Mine owners intensely resisted their efforts, such as during Colorado's 1914

Ludlow Massacre, where workers of different racial and ethnic backgrounds had organized for the right to unionize, an eight-hour working day, enforcement of safety laws, and compensation for all work done, not just payment per ton of coal produced. (Miners had typically only been paid by tonnage of coal produced, not other work, such as digging mines or shoring up mine tunnels.) When the workers went on strike, they were evicted from company housing and lived in tents provided by the United Mine Workers Union. Using machine guns, the Colorado National Guard and company guards fired on a tent where twelve hundred miners and their families lived, killing twenty-one and injuring more than five hundred others. Among the dead were Mexican, Black, Chinese, Italian, Greek, Slovenian, and British workers, as well as women and children who were family members.

The Ludlow Massacre reveals the complex connection between class, race, ethnicity, and labor. Management often used Black, Latino, Chinese, and Native American workers as strike-breakers, fueling the fires of racism. Race riots were common during the early part of the twentieth century. There were so many race riots in 1919 that Black author and civil rights leader James Weldon Johnson (also the author of the Black national anthem) dubbed the period "Red Summer."

During this volatile time, hundreds of Black people and some Whites were killed during riots in cities and rural areas all around the nation. The highest number of deaths occurred near the small town of Elaine, Arkansas, where an estimated 100–240 Black people were killed in the summer of 1919. Unlike the race riots of the 1960s that usually started from a confrontation between the police and Black people, the riots of 1919 typically began when White workers attacked Black people. Class conflict fractured the relationship between management and labor, but as Whites tried to hold on to their place, race split this fracture even further.

Now, the relationship between class and race has taken new form again. In the earlier industrial economy, people of color and

White workers, even those without an advanced education, could find relatively stable jobs with decent wages in manufacturing. The post–World War II shift from a manufacturing-based to a service-based economy has now robbed workers of the opportunities industrial jobs once provided.

"Rust Belt" cities such as Detroit, Cleveland, and Pittsburgh, to name a few, have been decimated as their foundational economy has disappeared. When such cities have rebounded, it has been through investment in new industries, such as tech companies, banking, and service-based industries. In the new postindustrial economy, different kinds of workers are needed—namely, those with more education and advanced technological skills. Without such skills, workers pay the price. Industrial jobs, such as in steel manufacturing, automobile assembly, and coal mining, have largely vanished, despite national promises to bring them back. Areas as diverse as Appalachia, where coal was the main industry, the American Southwest, where mining once prevailed, and Detroit, where automobile manufacturing was anchored, are places where workers have been largely dispossessed.

In a postindustrial economy, people without higher education or sophisticated technological skills get stuck in low-wage service work—or they may find no work at all. Robots or sophisticated technological devices do the work human hands once provided. Many workers feel abandoned, not without reason. Jobs that were once the stepping-stones to economic stability and the relative prosperity of the middle class are gone, not only for people of color but also for much of the White working-class. Sadly, despite their shared economic plight, race all too often still divides these workers.

The displacement of labor under this economic transformation has affected all groups, but it has been a unique hardship for those whose economic status was already tenuous. For many, a lifetime of low-wage work, or worse, chronic unemployment and poverty are the result. The result has been the growth of an *underclass*, largely, but not exclusively, urban and comprised mostly of people of color and recent immigrants. Shifts in the economic system have changed the connection between class and race. Class remains highly significant, but people of color feel the unique impact of race as well. Either class or race might appear to be more prominent at times, but they work together in shaping people's chances of success.

Class and race inequality are also intermingled with gender inequality. Isolating any one of them misses how they work together to shape people's lives. In what is now called intersectional theory, scholars have shown that no one of these social facts singularly determines anyone's lived experiences.[11] Obviously, not all White men are equally powerful nor are all people of color disadvantaged. Class is highly significant in determining one's overall well-being, but it does not operate absent the influence of race and gender too.

Any one person's or group's experience depends on the particular configuration of all these factors as they intersect at different points in time. It has taken the writing and work of women of color, in particular, to recognize the significance of intersectional thought. Without it, as an early team of Black women intellectuals wrote, "All the women are White, all the Blacks are men, but some of us are brave."[12]

The point is not to compare and rank oppressions or to try to discern whether race or class or gender is the most important feature of one's life. Rather, the point is to understand how race, class, *and* gender simultaneously overlap and interconnect to form inequality, shaping all people's lives, including those of White people.

Of course, at any given moment, a given person might feel the influence of one social factor more than another. A Black man stopped by the police in an affluent neighborhood will certainly feel the salience of his race most prominently at that moment. Likewise, a Latina who is sexually harassed while walking down the street will keenly feel her gender, but her identity as Latina merges both her gender and racial-ethnic identity, especially in how racialized gender stereotypes define her in sexual terms.

Together race, class, and gender create particular social and economic outcomes. What it means to be a woman—that is, how a woman is perceived, her life opportunities, and her own self-conception—differs depending on her race and class and gender position in society. White women are disadvantaged by virtue of their gender but are at the same time advantaged by virtue of their race.

Likewise, masculinity may be expressed or defined differently for a poor Latino man than for a Black middle-class man or a White working-class man. Intersectionality means race, class, and gender are not isolated one from the other. Each is manifested differently depending on its configuration with others. Understanding the interconnections of race, class, and gender is a more complete view of how society is organized, how we live our lives, how we perceive others, and how we perceive ourselves—all depending on our social location in an interlocking system of inequalities.

"Immigrants Are Taking Jobs from Americans and Getting Benefits Others Should Have"

Most people understand the United States is a nation of immigrants. With the exception of Native Americans, Black descendants of slaves, and Mexican Americans whose Southwestern land was seized by Anglos, everyone in this nation comes from an immigrant experience. The United States has more immigrants as a proportion of its population than any other nation in the world. Twenty percent of the US population is foreign-born, a total of nearly forty-four million people. Of that 20 percent, only one-quarter are unauthorized immigrants—a mere 3 percent of the total population.

China and India now surpass Mexico as the source of new immigrants. Yet Mexican and Central American immigrants are being vilified as overrunning the country—even though the number of Mexicans returning to Mexico from the United States now outpaces the number coming in.[13] The condemnation of Latino immigrants as "hordes" and a peril to the nation repeats earlier twentieth-century vilification of Asian immigrants. Now, however, Asians are stereotyped as hardworking overachievers driven by "tiger Moms."

The relative success of earlier White, European immigrants makes many believe that immigrants who try hard enough will succeed through hard work and developing the correct cultural values. The relative historic success of White European immigrants—and the class status of some Asian immigrant groups—has become the standard by which other immigrant groups are now being judged. The refrain is, "Other immigrant groups have made it. Why can't they?"

Lost in this perception is that each immigrant group faces different conditions as they enter the United States. New immigrants may be scorned for not adopting American culture and holding on to their own cultural values, such as when former news anchor Tom Brokaw said, "I also happen to believe that the Hispanics should work harder at assimilation . . . and make sure that all their kids are learning to speak English, and that they feel comfortable in their communities." Brokaw awkwardly apologized after his comment went viral on social media. What he said, though, echoes common anti-immigrant narratives.

How well different immigrant groups assimilate into society depends on a number of factors. Timing matters. White ethnics who arrived in the late nineteenth and early twentieth centuries came when the national economy was expanding. Although European immigrants experienced intense ethnic prejudice and sometimes outright racism, the nation needed workers. White European immigrants filled niches in the labor market where they could get a foothold in a growing economy.

The social and economic conditions a group encounters as they enter the United States matters in a group's likelihood of success. The skills and resources they bring with them also make a difference. And it matters if someone comes voluntarily as compared to Latinos whose land was annexed following war or Black Americans who arrived in the chains of slavery.

Some immigrant groups also arrive with strong government support. The immigration of Cubans into the United States in the 1960s is a good example. Cuban professionals and middle-class workers fled to the United States during the Cuban revolution when the Cuban government nationalized American industries on the island. Those Cubans who could afford to leave did so, and the United States welcomed them with an open-door policy. The prevalent anti-communist sentiment in the United States gave Cubans a more welcoming entrance than most other groups experienced. Although they were an exiled people and much of their property had been seized by the Cuban government, the first wave of Cubans who came never had to fear deportation. They were also eligible for government relief and had an easier path to citizenship than most other immigrants have had.

Once in the United States, different immigrant groups also experience distinct social and economic trajectories. Those who arrive with professional skills may find high-paying jobs in industry or higher education, depending on whether immigration policies give preference to their occupational status. Many, though, experience downward mobility. Among Vietnamese, Korean, and West Indian immigrants, for example, are people who were highly educated professionals in their homelands but who end up working mostly in low-wage personal service occupations, such nail salons and restaurants where their skills and talents are ignored.

Two counter narratives about immigrants—one as worthy strivers and the other as undeserving scoundrels—teeter throughout the nation's history. On the one hand, immigrants are extolled as a central part of "the story of America," heralded for being driven to succeed and praised for the diversity they bring. On the other hand, immigrants are at times, such as now, vilified as "vermin," "an infestation," or violent criminals. This is especially true for immigrants who are "brown" or as was earlier the case, "yellow" or "black." While the national story extols the virtues of hard work and self-determination, it simultaneously derides immigrants as alien intruders who are taking jobs away from other, supposedly more worthy, Americans. Even people who are seeking asylum from violence in their nation of origin are maligned in this narrative as violent thugs. In the words of Donald Trump, the allegation is, "They're not sending us their best."

In the unworthy narrative, immigrants are portrayed as a threat to society—typically through being stereotyped as bringing drugs, disease, and violent crime. Even though research consistently shows that immigrants have a much lower crime rate than do native-born citizens or second- and third-generation immigrants, this narrative persists. No matter how widely reported it is that immigrants have a lower crime rate than others, this fact falls on deaf ears because racism is a more powerful narrative than the truth.

In the unworthy narrative, immigrants are also accused of taking generous government benefits. The truth is, immigrants who enter lawfully must reside as a legal resident for five years before having full access to public benefits.[14] However, lawful immigrants are eligible for Social Security because Social Security is deducted from their pay, as are state and federal income taxes. Immigrants generally, however, receive less income from Social Security than comparably situated native-born workers, mostly because of the fewer number of years they are likely to have worked. Because most immigrants, including about half of undocumented workers, pay local, state, and federal taxes, they also contribute billions of dollars to state and federal tax revenues.

Except in unusual circumstances, undocumented immigrants, including DACA holders, are *not eligible* to receive public benefits, including food stamps, Medicaid, Social Security income, or TANF. They are also ineligible for health care under the Affordable Care Act. Given these facts, it is simply untrue that immigrants come to the United States because of supposedly generous public benefits.

During periods of intense *nativism*—that is, the idea that only native-born people should bear full rights—immigrants are especially likely to become racialized (that is, defined in racial terms, such as being "brown"). When immigrants are perceived, even wrongly so, as displacing native-born Whites, nativism becomes especially vicious.

Throughout the nation's history, various immigrant groups have been subjected to the racism and xenophobia that nativism produces. Chinese workers during the late nineteenth century were subjected to a strong racial backlash and were called the "yellow peril." Ominous and threatening images of Chinese people were widely circulated through popular culture. Now, immigrants, especially "brown" ones—are accused of taking jobs from other Americans, even though few Americans want to do the work so many immigrants provide.

The national debate around immigration policy rages on. Years from now when we look back, will we have embraced the diversity immigration brings and will we have extended citizenship to those who so desperately seek it? Or will the uglier sentiments of protecting the alleged supremacy of supposed "native" groups prevail? As we learned from the Civil Rights Movement, gains will not come without struggle. It remains to be seen whether the nation will keep its promise to welcome "the tired, the poor and those longing to be free."

"My Uncle Was Turned Down for a Job because They Met a Quota with a Person of Color"

There may be no more contentious issue in discussions of race than the widespread perception that people of color get favoritism simply because of their race. Conversations such as the following are common: "My uncle [or fill in the blank with some other relative] was turned down for a job because they had to give it to a Black man." Or "Women of color have it made now because they fill a double quota." Or "Asians are getting all the slots in prestigious colleges."

The assumption is always the same: Some unnamed, but unqualified, person has taken a job (or a college admissions slot) from a more deserving White person. If you want to have a heated conversation, just utter the words "affirmative action." Reasonable people can disagree on the value of affirmative action, but it is virtually impossible to have a sober and informed discussion about it because it taps into deep-seated feelings that this is a meritocratic society—that is, a society where only merit matters and people are rewarded based solely on their individual effort.

Affirmative action was originally developed as a way to increase the representation of racial-ethnic minorities in federal employment. In 1965, President Lyndon Johnson required all federal contractors to file plans for hiring more minority employees. Later, in 1969, and perhaps surprising to many, it was Republican president Richard Nixon who added the requirement for federal employers to file goals and timetables for hiring minority employees. Nixon also added women as a protected class to be included in affirmative action plans. In other words, affirmative action promoted *race-conscious and gender-conscious methods* to achieve better representation of people of color in the workplace (and later, higher education).

Numerous misconceptions swirl around affirmative action as a policy and practice. The biggest misconception is that affirmative action is a quota system. In truth, current law governing affirmative action explicitly prohibits quotas or "set asides." Affirmative action does require employers to make specific efforts to recruit and hire people of color and women. In higher education, federally supported institutions must file plans for diversifying their student body and employees, including faculty. In both employment and education, the person so hired or admitted *must be qualified* for the position they take. Employers must also demonstrate fairness in hiring procedures. Prior to the implementation of affirmative action, it was perfectly legal to hire people without any advertisement or outreach other than to one's personal networks.

There have been many legal challenges to the principle of affirmative action. The first was in 1978 in the *Bakke* decision (*Regents of the University of California v. Bakke*). Allan Bakke was a White male who was denied admission to the University of California–Davis Medical School. At the time, the UC Davis Medical School had a "set aside" program, under which it reserved sixteen slots for minority applicants, out of one hundred admission slots. Bakke sued and ultimately took his case to the US Supreme Court. Using the equal protection clause of the Fourteenth Amendment, the Supreme Court ruled the campus *could not* use quotas when admitting students to medical school, but it *could* take race into account when reviewing medical applicants. In other words, race could be considered as part of an applicant's file (for example, considering the circumstances an applicant has overcome), but quotas are unconstitutional and there cannot be slots set aside for minority applicants.

To this day (at least as of the writing of this book), the *Bakke* decision remains the law of the land. It is been challenged a number of times, but unless the law changes—and there are numerous pending legal challenges—colleges *may take race into account when making admissions decisions, but they may not use racial quotas.*

Despite the controversy surrounding affirmative action, a majority of the public says affirmative action is a good thing when used to increase the number of Black and minority students on campuses. Support dwindles, however, when people are asked if admissions officers should consider race when making admissions decisions. Only 31 percent approve of doing so; two-thirds disapprove of such action. Interestingly, people are more likely to support affirmative action when it is applied to women than when applied to racial minority groups.[15]

Although many people believe affirmative action is unfair by giving preference to people of color, multiple groups have actually benefited from affirmative action. White women have been some of the most benefited. As White women have found better and more positions open to them, their families have benefited as well. Affirmative action programs have been most effective in opening access to well-educated and well-trained people. However, affirmative action does little to address other problems, such as the prevalence of low-wage work or high rates of joblessness and poverty among people of color. Still, there is little doubt that affirmative action has been one of the factors that have helped expand the African American and Latino middle class.

Whether affirmative action remains the law of land is yet to be seen. The ultimate outcome for affirmative action will be decided by the courts, most likely involving college admissions. In one case, a group of Asian Americans who were rejected by Harvard have sued, arguing that Harvard systematically discriminates against Asian Americans by not basing admissions solely on test scores and grades. Critics of this argument point out that universities have to consider multiple factors in admissions decisions to produce the best learning environment. Research shows, for example, that all students learn more when they are educated in a diverse environment.[16]

Further, many point out that other forms of preference always enter into admissions decisions, a fact starkly revealed in 2019 when several prominent celebrities and wealthy people were found guilty of violating federal laws against bribery because they paid bribes to get their children into competitive universities. Aside from these illegal acts, colleges routinely give preference to various groups, athletes and children of alumni especially. Relatives of donors are also often given preference in college admissions. Rarely are strict and quantifiable measures of merit (such as grades and test scores) the sole basis for college admission. Factors such as athletic ability, leadership skills, musical talent, overcoming early obstacles, and other more subjective skills, talents, and experiences are usually considered during the admissions process. As an admissions officer once told me, "Don't give me any more women applicants who play the piano or the violin: We need people to play woodwinds in the college orchestra."

At the heart of the legal tangle around affirmative action is whether race-blind or race-specific measures should be used to make employment and education decisions. Ironically, conservative activists have seized the language of liberals to argue that rights should not be based on particular characteristics, whether race, religion, gender, or national origin. Those on the other side of this argument purport that we are not a purely meritocratic society. That is, rarely does success come purely from individual effort. Americans extol those who rise to riches despite modest origins, even though it is relatively rare to do so. Most people end up in more or less the same socioeconomic position as their point of origin or worse, evidenced by people's current fears that they will not fare as well as their parents. The national debate over affirmative action may well come to an end, depending on future court decisions, but the sentiments driving this debate are likely here to stay.

Systemic Racism: It Isn't New

For a while, especially in the aftermath of the election of Barack Obama as president of the United States, it seemed the United States had reached a sort of détente about race relations. Some even thought we were living in a "post-racial" society. Although that idea has been largely debunked by those attuned to the workings of racism, there is, at least in polite company, a sense that expressing overt racism is wrong or something we might be overcoming. Of late, though, frequent outbursts of overt racism have been screaming for our attention.

Following the election of Donald Trump as president, there was a surge in the number of reported hate crimes across the nation. In addition to the Charlottesville, Virginia, "Unite the Right" White supremacy march that ended in tragedy in August 2017, millions were heartbroken when a forty-six-year-old White man, Robert Gregory Bowers, an avowed white nationalist, walked into a synagogue in Pittsburgh during services in October 2018 and massacred eight people, injuring several others. In January 2019, Republican congressman Steve King was removed from all his committee assignments in the US House of Representatives soon after he said, "White nationalist, white supremacist, Western civilization—how did that language become offensive?" Around the same time, Virginia's Democratic governor was denounced when a photograph of someone, maybe him, dressed in blackface and standing with someone dressed in Ku Klux Klan garb was discovered in his 1984 medical school yearbook.

These and other horrendous events, such as the massacre in El Paso in 2019, remind us that these forms of hatred are alive and well. They have stunned people. Quite frequently, you hear people saying, "I'm shocked by the racism we are seeing now. This is not America!" But is this America? In fact, it is. Racism is the ugly part of our national story that, although it has recently caught some people off guard, has been with us all along.

Yes, something truly ugly has surfaced but it is not new. It might help to think of systemic racism as the embers in a smoldering fire—still burning, though not very visible. All it takes is one spark to ignite the fire. The spark might be a president who says a judge presumed to be of Mexican origin is biased because of his race. Or it might be just the slow burn of racial resentment—the widespread sentiment that White people are losing out while people of color supposedly have it made.

However you look at it, racism is persistent and dogged. The anti-Semitic, anti-Muslim, anti-immigrant, and racist comments and actions we are witnessing now are deeply alarming. Statements and acts of hatred reveal a vein of racial animosity and tension deep within our nation's foundation. People may be shocked by seeing how vicious racism and anti-Semitism are now, but they are not new.

The different refrains of racism we have examined here form a narrative about race that is hard to dislodge. They have several things in common. First is the idea that individual effort is the basis for success. Whether it is poor women of color, the urban underclass, immigrants, affirmative action beneficiaries, or any other group of people, blaming the victim attributes the cause of racial inequality to individual people's values, cultural outlooks, and supposed bad choices. The implication is that all we need to do is change the people who are most harmed by racism and inequality and we will all be better off.

Second, the narrative power of these racial refrains is bolstered by the belief that America is a meritocracy—one where people can rise regardless of their origins. Whether coming into the nation from different lands or working one's way out of poverty, hard work is perceived as the key to success. Popular legends extol the virtues of people who have become wildly successful even when starting from modest origins. People like Oprah Winfrey, Tiger Woods, and Barack and Michelle Obama come to mind. No doubt about it: These are people with remarkable talent whose hard work and dedication to their craft have made them very wealthy, despite their modest backgrounds. Such cases, though, are the exception, not the rule. Most people end up in much the same class where they began. Equally true is that far more people with great talent and intelligence never soar to such heights.

Racist refrains also rest on an implicit assumption that some people are more deserving than others. This dichotomy between the worthy and the undeserving serves one primary purpose: lifting the perceived value of those who already hold more advantaged positions while keeping others down.

Each of these racial refrains ignores the systematic character of racial inequality and how racism supports inequality. For a time, racism seemed to be marginalized into certain fringes of society, but we are seeing now how much a part of our nation's core institutions racism actually is. This realization begs the question: How did we get here and what can we do to change it?—subjects for the next two chapters.

CHAPTER 5

But That Was Then—I Didn't Have Anything to Do with It

The great force of history comes from the fact that we carry it within us, are unconsciously controlled by it in many ways, and history is literally present in all we do.

—JAMES BALDWIN[1]

MANY PEOPLE THINK THAT PRESENT-DAY ATTITUDES EXPLAIN racial inequality, yet, at the same time, no one thinks they are guilty of having created it. How often have you heard someone say, "I know slavery was terrible, but my family didn't do it. That has nothing to do with me." "What happened to Native American people was awful, but there is nothing I can do about that now." Or "Segregation was really bad, but I wasn't even born then. It's not my fault." "We are past all that. People should just get over it."

Such statements reveal a fundamental conundrum in the public's understanding of racial inequality. The signs of racial inequality are readily apparent to anyone who looks, but no one thinks it is their fault. In a certain way, people are right: Many of the reasons for racial inequality precede the lives and actions of people today, but policies and practices from the past, along with contemporary actions, frame the inequality we see today. Because this is not always obvious, people instead tend to blame some presumed "other"—either individual racists or people with supposedly bad values, as we saw in the previous chapter.

The past, however, continues to influence the present in ways that attitudes cannot explain. Of course, attitudes matter, and people can take individual responsibility for challenging individual racists, but without changing the societal conditions that have produced racial inequality, including the consequences of past racist practices, racial inequality will persist. Individual changes are not enough. We also have to imagine actions and policies that can alter the course of the history to come.

You can see the impact of the past by considering the following scenario. Imagine two couples looking to buy their first home. Each is a married couple with two young children. All four parents have full-time jobs and hold college degrees. The two couples have the same household income and they work in comparable jobs. In other words, their income, educational credentials, employment status, and family structure are the same. The only difference is that one couple is White, and the other is African American.

As each couple begins their search for a new home, they work with a real estate agent who is glad to show them properties they can afford. The agent shows the White couple homes in a mostly White, middle-income neighborhood where there are good schools nearby. The homes they see are affordable for first-time home buyers and are predicted to increase in value over time.

The agent shows the African American couple homes they can afford in a racially integrated neighborhood where the houses are large but showing their age. The nearest schools are "majority-minority"—that is, attended mostly by Black and Latino students. When the couple asks why they were shown houses in this neighborhood, the agent says, "I thought you would prefer to be in this kind of neighborhood with people like you." As the couple later learns, houses in this area have recently depreciated. The neighborhood is changing from being racially integrated to becoming mostly Black and Latino with a few older White residents who have lived there for a long time.

Racial attitudes are clearly part of this scenario, as when the real estate agent said the African American couple would prefer to live in an integrated neighborhood with "people like them." The agent is also biased in assuming the White couple would prefer a mostly White neighborhood. Other assumptions might also be at play: Did you think of the mostly White neighborhood as racially segregated? Probably not, but it is. Racial attitudes tend to mark neighborhoods as "racially segregated" only when they are mostly Black or Latino. All-white neighborhoods are somehow perceived as just "neighborhoods." Individual attitudes are a part of this imaginary scenario, but other things are happening here that have little to do with individual attitudes and have everything to do with racial inequities that predate either couple's decision to buy a home.

Take this hypothetical scenario one step further: The couples eventually buy houses with the same purchasing price, but the African American couple ends up with a higher monthly payment. How can this happen? The Fair Housing Act of 1968 prohibits discrimination against people who are renting or buying a home. Yet, two families, comparable in terms of income, education, occupation, and family structure end up with different monthly payments. Perhaps the White couple used an inheritance or gift from their parents that allowed them to make a substantial down payment, thus lowering their monthly cost. Maybe the African American couple had more debt from student loans. If so, the lending institution might have charged them a higher interest rate because they are seen as a greater financial risk.

Aside from these factors, other things will affect each couple's financial obligation and the value of their home over time. It is well demonstrated in research that neighborhoods tend to decline in value when they change from being mostly White—or even racially integrated—to being predominately African American and/or Latino. Although each couple might purchase a home with the same initial value, if the White couple buys in a mostly White neighborhood, their home is likely to increase in value over time. On the other hand, if the African American couple buys in an integrated or mostly Black or Latino neighborhood, their home's value could well decline in value over time. In other words, the White couple's equity will likely increase while the African American couple's equity may decrease—or, at least, not appreciate as much. This result is through no fault of their own.

In this not-so-hypothetical scenario, factors well beyond attitudes, individual preferences, and current economic status affect the current financial standing for each couple and the home equity they will build over time. Even with all things otherwise equal and laws in place that protect against discrimination, past actions and policies that go well beyond individual attitudes continue to influence the economic standing of different racial and ethnic groups today. This is apparent in racial patterns of income and wealth.

Accumulating Advantage and Disadvantage

Federal data show a significant income gap between White, Black, and Hispanic Americans. Further, that gap has hardly changed over the past fifty years—a period when civil rights protections were in place. Although income levels have risen for all groups over time, the gap between White Americans and everyone else has hardly budged (see figure 5.1). Among Asian Americans household income exceeds that of Whites, but the national data sources do not usually distinguish different Asian groups, such as Japanese, Chinese, Filipino, Cambodian, Vietnamese, Asian Indian, and other Asian American people. There are, however, substantial income differences among these different groups. For example, Bangladeshi, Hmong, and Burmese Americans have household incomes far below the national median and poverty among Cambodian and Hmong people, as two examples, closely matches that of African Americans and Latinos.[2]

As significant as income differences are in describing racial inequality, racial disparities in wealth are even more glaring (see

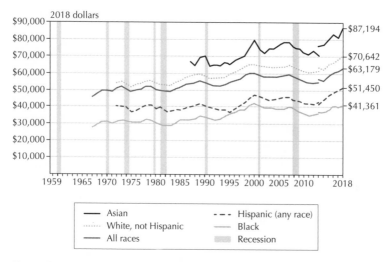

Figure 5.1. Real Median Household Income by Race and Hispanic Origin, 1967–2018. *Source:* Jessica Semega, Melissa Kollar, John Creamer, and Abinash Mohanty, *Income and Poverty in the United States: 2018* (Washington, DC: U.S. Census Bureau, Current Population Survey, 1968–2018; Report Number P60-266, Table A-2, "Households by Total Money Income, Race, and Hispanic Origin of Householder: 1967 to 2018," https://census.gov/library/publications/2019/demo/p60-266.html (accessed October 4, 2019).

Note: Because of changes in how the census has defined and enumerated different racial and ethnic groups, data for the category "white, non-Hispanic" were referred to as "white" from 1967 through 1971; Asians were not delineated until 2002; Hispanics, in 1972. Note, too, that given the Census checkoff, Hispanics can also be included in any of the races noted here.

figure 5.2). Wealth is the value of all of one's financial assets minus debt. The result is one's net worth—or wealth. Wealth works like frequent flyer miles: The more you have, the more you get. Having even a modest amount of wealth can help pay for your children's education or give you preferred status when applying for loans. Even small savings help in an emergency, such as job loss, a health crisis, or a natural disaster. Unlike income, wealth can accumulate over time, generates additional resources, and can be passed on to heirs. As a result, current generations may benefit from investments made several generations ago. Likewise, if one's ancestors

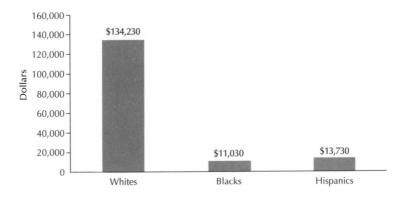

Figure 5.2. The Wealth Gap. *Source:* Signe-Mary McKernan, Caroline Ratcliffe, E. Eugene Steuerie, Emma Kalish, and Caleb Quakenbush, *Nine Charts about Wealth Inequality in America* (Washington, DC: Urban Institute, 2015), http://apps.urban.org/features/wealth-inequality-charts (accessed May 21, 2019).

were closed out of investment opportunities in days gone by, the current generation will be less well off.

The consequence of this reality is that, currently, White Americans, on average, have *twelve times* the wealth of Black Americans and *ten times* as much as Latinos. Another way to put this is that for every dollar held by White Americans, African Americans have nine cents; Latinos, ten cents. Further, the racial wealth gap remains even at comparable income levels. African Americans living at the median income level (in 2016) have, on average, $17,000 in net worth (including home equity). Latinos have $21,000. In contrast, White Americans at this same income level have $171,000, on average, in net worth.

White Americans also have significantly more wealth than other groups even at comparable levels of education. With only a high school education, Whites have average wealth of $78,300 compared to $3,200 for Black Americans. At higher levels of education, the wealth gap remains. Whites with post-college degrees have an average of $293,100 in wealth; Blacks, $84,000. And among parents, White single parents have twice as much wealth as either Black or Latino two-parent families.[3]

The racial differences in wealth are staggering. Many factors influence this stark reality, persistent income inequality being one of them. Obviously, higher incomes make it possible to save and invest more, and differences earned over a lifetime add up. But you cannot explain the wealth gap without understanding the impact of race-specific practices from the past.

Sociologists Melvin Oliver and Thomas Shapiro have coined the term *sedimentation of racial inequality* to capture the idea that past racial discrimination continues to have a deleterious effect in the present.[4] Even were there no discrimination now, well-documented past practices have suppressed the ability of people of color to experience economic mobility. Obviously, there are exceptions and such individual success stories are widely extolled. But the sedimentation of racial inequality has retarded the upward mobility of many African American and Latino families.

Numerous examples of local, state, and federal government actions explain the persistent racial wealth gap. Further, many of these government actions were developed specifically *because of race*, robbing people of color of the same opportunities that many White Americans had. The federal New Deal, implemented under Franklin Delano Roosevelt's administration to alleviate the effects of the Great Depression in the 1930s, provides the first example.

New Deal programs did not explicitly deny benefits to Black citizens, but in effect, they did. The Social Security Act of 1935 (part of the New Deal) would never have cleared Congress without the support of southern Democrats who staunchly supported white supremacy. To get their votes, Congress reached a compromise that denied Social Security benefits to domestic and agricultural workers. Consequently, if you were Black in the 1930s, given where most Black people were then employed, odds are you were denied the Social Security benefits most White people could receive. Whose rights were compromised?

Throughout the mid-twentieth century, numerous government actions prevented people of color from investing in property that could have improved their economic status in years to come. As more Americans began to buy homes, rather than renting, many were able to achieve a landmark of the American dream: owning one's own home. Redlining denied people of color this significant asset. A common practice beginning in the 1930s, redlining refers to actual red lines drawn on government maps that marked minority neighborhoods as hazardous for investment. Green lines color-coded an area as "best." Blue lines meant "still desirable"; yellow lines meant "in decline."

The practice of redlining especially affected Black and Mexican neighborhoods, and also restricted investment in areas where Catholic, Jewish, southern European, and Asian immigrants resided. Researchers have looked back at government maps drawn in the 1930s and found that three out of four such neighborhoods were redlined. Although redlining was outlawed as a form of discrimination by the Fair Housing Act of 1968, more than fifty years later, its effects remain. Today, most of the areas redlined in the 1930s are now low-income Black and Latino neighborhoods, while almost all the neighborhoods earlier classified as "best" are now predominately White and middle to upper income.[5]

During the post–World War II period, the federal government also made massive investments in building new suburbs, providing subsidies to alleviate the postwar housing shortage and to support real estate developers and banks. With government support and a modest income, a White family could purchase a small home with little or no mortgage interest, often with no down payment. In fact, by the late 1940s, most new housing was constructed with government financing,[6] a startling fact given that many of the same families whose ancestors benefited from this "government handout" now recoil at the idea of government support for people of color.

Suburban development was a huge boon to White working- and middle-class families. The burgeoning suburbs, however, excluded Black and Mexican families, usually through explicit race-based regulations. Zoning restrictions; restrictive covenants that were common in mortgage deeds; community association rules specifically excluding Black and Mexican families; redlining; and other exclusionary practices spurred suburban growth for Whites but produced much of the racial segregation we still live with today.[7]

Racial covenants written into housing deeds were common throughout the United States, such as in the St. Ann suburb of St. Louis, where deeds prohibited selling, leasing, or being occupied by anyone "other than those of the Caucasian race."[8] In the planned community of Levittown, New York, *every* home had such a racial covenant in its deed. The impact of such exclusion is still felt today: A house bought in Levittown for $8,000 in the late 1940s ($75,000 in today's dollars) would today be worth $350,000, even with no upgrades. No Black or Mexican family would have been able to buy such a home in the 1940s—not in Levittown or in the many all-White suburbs that were developed throughout the nation with comparable exclusions. A White working-class family who bought such a house in the 1940s would have gained $200,000 in wealth three generations later.[9]

Now, even with racial discrimination being legally outlawed, it is harder for people with modest means to gain a foothold in the home ownership market. Houses that were once affordable to those with modest incomes are now unaffordable to many, regardless of race. But you can imagine how much less of a racial wealth gap there would be had Black and Latino families been more easily able to invest in property years ago. That early investment, denied to so many, would have secured a much stronger financial base for current generations. This is how the past still matters.

Other government policies have had similarly detrimental effects for people of color. Even when not overtly discriminatory, the reality of systemic racism has robbed people of color of past opportunities for economic security. The GI Bill provides an example. Passed in the aftermath of World War II, the GI Bill was intended to retrain and provide opportunities for returning veterans. It provided access to low-cost home mortgages, business loans, and education. Under the GI Bill, you could get a very low-interest home loan, perhaps without making a down payment. These starter homes appreciated over the years, giving their owners some degree of financial equity—an asset they could reinvest or pass on to their heirs.

Who benefited? African Americans and other people of color were among those who fought in World War II and were technically entitled to the benefits of the GI Bill. But systemic racism prevented people of color from accessing the opportunities this important legislation provided. In many places, local officials who administered the distribution of GI benefits were bigots who endorsed white supremacy, making it difficult, if not impossible, for Black veterans to access the benefits of this law.

As the GI Bill was providing World War II veterans with unprecedented access to higher education, racial segregation kept Black veterans out of most collegiate institutions—certainly in the South, but also in the North where they were a tiny proportion of students in the most selective institutions. Although the GI Bill provided a boon for enrollment in historically Black colleges, racial segregation in education remained a fact of life. As a result, the educational benefits that so many Whites received through the GI Bill were far less available to Black and Mexican veterans. Even though current descendants of World War II veterans might not readily recognize the advantages the GI Bill provided, historians now say that it was the single most important factor in creating America's White middle class—what has been called "affirmative action for Whites."[10]

Time and time again, government policies failed people of color. Even when policies appear to have been race-blind, people of color have paid the price. In another example, you probably do not think of the federal interstate highway system as racially biased. The interstate highway system, first built in the 1950s, was designed to reduce city traffic, increase interstate commerce, and facilitate the movement of people from the developing suburbs to city jobs—all noble intentions seemingly void of racial bias. Everyone uses the interstate system. No one is denied access to it. Everyone takes it for granted. The interstate roads let us move relatively easily from place to place, state to state, and coast to coast. And yet, the interstate highway system has had deleterious effects on many communities where people of color live.

In many places, highways were built in ways that actually walled off Black and Latino urban neighborhoods—something you can still see in many places if you look. Because Blacks and Mexicans were kept out of suburban areas, they were also less well-served by federally funded transportation. Many were cut off from transportation networks that provided access to jobs in more economically vital parts of the city. The cost of the new highway system also strained the transportation budgets of cities, where many people of color remained, thus reducing city services. There was also a shift in the balance of power between cities and suburbs. Whereas Whites could prosper in the newly developed suburbs, people of color were cordoned off by this large federal investment in transportation.

All told, people denied opportunities in the past simply start from a different place in the present even when formal obstacles have been removed. Too little, too late means the playing field is just not level. Excluded from past government support before, people cannot catch up. Add to that the fact that housing is now more expensive and takes a larger share of one's monthly income and you have a recipe for persistent racial inequality.

President Lyndon Johnson well captured the impact of the past in a famous commencement address delivered at Howard University in 1965. He said, "You do not take a person who, for years, has been hobbled by chains and liberate him, bring him up to the starting line of a race and then say, 'You are free to compete with all the others,' and still justly believe that you have been completely fair."[11] As the opening scenario of this chapter illustrates, many factors—past and present—influence different outcomes for people of color today.

WORKING FOR THE BENEFIT OF OTHERS

Even as they were being denied opportunities to secure their financial future, people of color built much of the wealth and well-being of others. They are not the only ones to have done so, but without the labor of people of color, the United States would not be the affluent society it is today. Architectural icons of American society—the White House, the US Capitol, the Empire State Building, Rockefeller Center in New York, and the fallen World Trade Center towers—were constructed using African American, Native American, Latino, *and* White working-class hands.

Beginning with slavery, the labor of different racial and ethnic groups has had a profound impact on who has accumulated property and who has not. What work people did, under what conditions, and how they were rewarded—or not—form the tapestry of our nation's labor history—a history very much marked by racial inequality. In some cases, people came to the United States to find work and opportunity. Others arrived in chains, providing work that built the nation's economy. Slavery, indentured servitude, contract labor, convict labor: All are part of our national story. People of color generated property—sometimes for themselves, but more typically for the benefit of others. You cannot understand the current realities of race in America without having at least a brief understanding of the history of racial labor.

As historian Peter Kolchin has written, slavery in the United States provided the "bedrock of the economy and of the social order."[12] Other societies have had slaves, but only in the Americas did slavery develop into a full-blown social and economic institution. Precolonial African nations, for example, depended on slave labor, but in African societies slaves could marry free people and their children did not automatically become slaves, as was the case in the United States. Only in the West (including the United States, Latin America, and the Caribbean) were slaves defined as *chattel*—that is, they and their children and their children's children, along with all descendants, were the lifetime property of others.

Some of the earliest White settlers in what became the United States were also bound to employers, but as indentured servants. In the early days of the Virginia colony, for example, most workers were White indentured servants (an estimated 75 percent of those arriving in the seventeenth century). Indentured servants, though, received some form of economic compensation, and there was a time limit on their servitude. Further, unlike under slavery, should an indentured servant have children, the children were not owned. Some of the earliest indentured servants were Black, who shared the exploitation of White workers. Historical records show that White and Black indentured servants sometimes even ran away together. Over time, however, Black servants saw their condition worsen, culminating in what became the institution of slavery.[13]

Slaves provided the free labor that built wealth both for the southern plantation class and for Northern industrialists who benefited from the trade in tobacco, wheat, rice, and—later—cotton. Slavery developed even as the nation extolled the principles of freedom, independence, and the "natural rights of man." How could people reconcile this fundamental contradiction in their professed beliefs—that is, holding human beings as property while promoting the rights of man?

The answer is racism. Believing that Black people were somehow different, not fully human, allowed White people to justify to themselves one of the cruelest systems of economic and political power. Reconciling this inhumanity with the ideals of the new nation is epitomized in the political compromise between northern and southern interests to count Black slaves, for purposes of

Congressional representation, as only three-fifths of a person, with none of the rights or privileges afforded White men.

Although only a small number of White southern families actually owned slaves, the institution of slavery concentrated power in the South in the hands of a White aristocracy. Both the planter class and the northern industrialists who benefited from slavery wielded enormous political and economic power. White workers had little power in this system, but racist ideologies prevented them from seeing any common interests with Black workers.

With the end of the Civil War, the Southern economy was ravaged, functioning like a colony of the North. Although Black Americans in the South enjoyed some degree of freedom and the rights of citizenship during Reconstruction, the compromise between northern and southern congressmen that ended Reconstruction in 1890 brought new terrors to previously enslaved people. Practically overnight, Black rights were stripped and a new era of racial oppression began. When the boll weevil infestation decimated the cotton crop—the primary economic driver in the South—hundreds of thousands of workers, Black and White, were left without agricultural work. Many relocated to southern cities in search of new opportunities.

Meanwhile, by the early twentieth century, the rapidly industrializing North needed more workers, a need exacerbated when World War I reduced the flow of European immigrants. Northern industrialists actively recruited Black workers from the South, at the same time that Black people were seeking better economic and social opportunities and trying to escape the ravages of Jim Crow segregation. The result was one of the greatest population movements in the nation's history—the Great Migration. From 1916 to 1930, approximately one million African American people left the South and headed to northern and midwestern cities, including Chicago, Detroit, New York and Pittsburgh. As the Great Migration continued, southern authorities tried desperately to halt this mass exodus by arresting labor agents, fining migrants and labor agents, and even going so far as to stop trains to pull Black migrants off.

While northern migration brought great hope to African Americans—and brought rich talent to the nation's largest cities—their hopes were dashed; previously skilled workers were shunted into low-wage work and put into overt and fierce competition with White workers. Some African American men moved into industrial work; others found only unskilled, often seasonal, work. Black women found steady employment, but usually as private domestic workers—work that was steady but severely underpaid. In 1920, for example, 41 percent of Black women in the nation worked as private servants and 20 percent as laundry workers. As late as 1940, two-thirds of employed Black women were still working as private domestic workers.

African American dreams of finding a better world in the North were dashed, but not forgotten, even as Black people encountered new forms of racism in the North. Under the most trying conditions, Black people organized for change and brought newly vitalized Black culture to American life in the form of the Harlem Renaissance of the 1920s. The concentration of Black talent in places like Harlem, but also in other cities, created artistic oases. To this day, legendary greats such as Jacob Lawrence, Langston Hughes, Billie Holiday, Duke Ellington, Zora Neale Hurston, and many more created a treasure trove of art, literature, and music that now defines a core part of American culture. The Great Migration is a prime example of how structural forces of society combine and interact with the efforts, talents, and desires of ordinary people to change the course of history.[14]

Other groups in the history of American racial labor have similar stories—having their work usurped for the benefit of others even while people resist their exploitation and find resilience under conditions of great oppression. Mexican, Chinese, Japanese, and other American minorities have been among some of the most significant economic drivers in US history, but in every case, they have organized however they could to resist and change the social forces of their situations.

The original settlers in California, in addition to Native Indians, were Mexicans whose social order was marked by an elaborate class system. Some were elite landowners and prosperous officials. In the middle of this class system were small-scale ranchers and farmers. At the bottom were laborers, artisans, and other skilled workers, many of whom were Indians, although their numbers were diminishing as the result of genocide and disease.[15]

The Mexican government had outlawed slavery in 1830, but southern cotton planters in the United States were anxious to expand into what became Texas—originally held as Mexican territory. The infamous battle at the Alamo began when armed Whites began an insurrection against Mexican authority. A brutal military campaign followed, eventually leading to the Mexican-American War of 1846–1848. Outgunned, the Mexican government lost the war and signed the Treaty of Guadalupe Hidalgo.

With this treaty, Mexico ceded over one million square miles to the United States, extending the southern US border to the Rio Grande. That land now includes the states of Texas, California, New Mexico, Nevada, and parts of Colorado, Arizona, and Utah—an area that was roughly half of what had been Mexico. Overnight, the fifty thousand or so Mexicans living in these areas were declared to be US citizens and were given citizenship rights—at least in principle, if not in practice.[16] As some say today, "We didn't cross the border; the border crossed us."

Because of the Gold Rush of 1848, people throughout the United States headed west, thinking they would become wealthy from prospecting. Soon, the Anglo population overwhelmed the Mexican American population, and Mexican Americans found themselves thoroughly subjected to Anglo domination. Laws and other ordinances were put in place that restricted Mexican American rights. Those who had been landed often became landless. Many Mexican ranchers who had held large tracts of land moved from "riches to rags" while Anglos increasingly controlled the new economic system.[17] Lands were seized, and Mexican Americans were targeted for all manner of abuse. Moreover, people who were once indigenous to the United States became defined in racial terms and were subjected to all the indignities that racism hurls at people.[18]

As the economic base of the nation expanded, there was an increasing need for laborers. Cheap labor, especially, enriched the profits of business owners. Growers and industrialists recruited people from far and wide, spending thousands to recruit and transport Mexicans to where their work was needed, including such far-flung places as Colorado, Wyoming, Iowa, Nebraska, and even the city of Chicago. Ranching, agriculture, and mining drew many Mexicans to the Southwest. With virtually no immigration laws, Mexicans and others found it relatively easy to migrate to the land that was now the United States. Employers heavily recruited Mexican laborers, greatly increasing the rate of immigration from Mexico to the United States. The number of Mexican immigrants jumped from about seventeen thousand per year in 1910 to about fifty thousand per year in the 1920s and seven hundred forty thousand by 1930.[19]

As the Mexican population grew, White opposition intensified, and by the late 1920s when the Great Depression hit, Mexicans became the scapegoats for the failing US economy. A period of intense anti-Mexican hatred ensued. There was massive deportation of Mexicans during the Great Depression from 1929 to 1934. Authorities rounded up Mexicans through raids in neighborhoods, factories, and fields, often without a chance for people to gather their belongings. Steeped in anti-Mexican stereotypes, officials often did not distinguish Mexican immigrants from Mexican Americans who were US citizens. Thousands of children were also deported, regardless of their citizenship status. This massive deportation shrank the population of Mexicans in the United States by half.[20]

The indignities of having one's labor used for the benefit of others also marks the history of Asian American people. Harsh conditions in China during the nineteenth century, along with the settlement of California, encouraged many Chinese people to come to the United States. They saw the United States as a place where they could earn money and establish their homes. Men came to find work, thinking they would get established and then move their families.

Most Chinese people came through a "credit-ticket" system where a broker would lend them the money for passage. They were to repay it with interest from their earnings in the United States. Between 1850 and 1882, more than three hundred thousand Chinese people left southern China to work in America. Many were imported specifically to work as strikebreakers because White laborers were protesting exploitative working conditions. Chinese workers were routinely relegated to the most dangerous and difficult work.[21]

Few Chinese women came to the United States during this time. Women's traditional roles in China, the cost of travel, and Chinese women's fears of sexual assault in the United States created a huge imbalance in the ratio of men to women among the Chinese in America. As one example, of the 11,787 Chinese who came to the United States in 1852, only seven were women. Some Chinese women managed to enter as indentured servants, but the extreme sex imbalance created bachelor communities and a lucrative market for prostitution, especially since California law prevented Chinese people from marrying Whites. In the 1870 census, 61 percent of Chinese women living in California listed their occupation as that of prostitute.[22]

At first, Chinese men worked mostly in the mining industry, but the decline of mining, the resistance of white labor, and the building of the transcontinental railroad changed the course of Chinese labor and immigration. Chinese railroad workers were an estimated 90 percent of those who built the transcontinental railroad—extremely dangerous and arduous work, especially as the track was laid to pass through the Sierra Nevada Mountains and then beyond into the rugged western landscape. Paid less than White workers, Chinese railroad workers were widely recruited by railroad owners who reaped the profits of this extraordinary work. Scholars estimate the work of Chinese railroad men to have saved owners one-third of their costs. At times, Chinese workers organized to demand equal pay and better working conditions, but their efforts were rebuffed by owners, often through violence and intimidation.

Once the railroad was completed in 1869, most of the Chinese workers returned to California, mostly to San Francisco and Sacramento, where they were concentrated in low-wage work and paid less than Whites even in the rare cases where they did the same work. Some turned to farming, where their labor developed the fruit and vegetable industry. Others, shut out of work opportunities, moved into service work, such as laundry work.[23]

By the 1880s, when there was no longer a need for Chinese workers, Chinese people in America, who had once been defined as ideal workers, were relabeled as a "yellow peril"—a menace to white society. Although the Chinese workers were, when needed, praised for their ingenuity and hard work, once the work was complete, they were reviled and ultimately barred from entering the United States. In 1882, Congress passed the Chinese Exclusion Act, barring entry of any Chinese laborers. The door of opportunity that had been briefly opened was now slammed shut. The only Chinese allowed entry to the United States were those who were merchants, teachers, diplomats, students, and tourists. Women could only enter if they were married to a merchant, a regulation that can help explain the somewhat higher-class status of Chinese people relative to other Asian groups. Not until 1943 were Chinese people allowed to become naturalized citizens.[24]

When the San Francisco earthquake of 1906 destroyed city records, some Chinese were able to reformulate families by claiming they had been born in San Francisco. They could then travel back to China, returning with those they claimed as sons—so-called *paper sons*. Not until 1943, when China and the United States became allies in World War II, was the Chinese Exclusion Act rescinded. Immigration restrictions that favored only a certain class of Chinese immigrants are one reason for the higher economic status of many Chinese Americans today.

Japanese immigration to the United States followed a different, though related course. Most Japanese immigration occurred between 1890 and 1924. Most of the first Japanese immigrants were men, but unlike among Chinese immigrants, Japanese women were far more likely to emigrate. The strong central Japanese government wanted Japan to appear "noble" to others and thus strictly regulated emigration, requiring those who left to be healthy and literate, thus representing Japanese society well. The Japanese government allowed Japanese women to emigrate only as family members.[25]

In the late nineteenth century, poor farming conditions in Japan meant that many farmers lost their land and crops. Like the Chinese, many Japanese people thought that coming to the United States would mean high wages and a more successful life. As with Chinese immigrants, immigration policies favored those who were somewhat better off, thus shaping the relative success of Japanese people in the United States.

While Chinese workers were being excluded, Japanese workers were initially welcomed. Between 1885 and 1924, two hundred thousand Japanese people emigrated to Hawaii and another one hundred eighty thousand to the US mainland, where they were a smaller proportion of the population. Unlike with the Chinese where women had been excluded, in Hawaii, the government stipulated that a certain percentage of workers had to be women. Once there, women were assigned to field work. On the mainland, women assisted husbands as unpaid workers in shops and as farmers.

Many Japanese believed that their success in agriculture would be the ticket to acceptance, but sadly they were wrong. Anti-immigrant sentiment in the United States began curtailing Japanese immigration. The Gentleman's Agreement of 1907—an agreement between the United States and Japan—barred further entry of Japanese laborers, significantly reducing Japanese immigratism. This agreement only allowed women to come as wives of merchants. The result was a system of *picture brides*—marriages arranged by a broker (as was the custom in Japan). A Japanese man in the United States who could not afford to return to Japan selected a wife from picture books provided by brokers. Between 1909 and 1923, 71 percent of the Japanese women arriving in the United States came as picture brides.[26]

Organized White US workers scorned and attacked Japanese workers, denying them access to industrial jobs where they might have been better off. Instead, Japanese workers were relegated to farming and in some cases, shopkeeping. By 1910, Japanese laborers in California were producing 70 percent of strawberries, 95 percent of soybeans, 95 percent of celery, and huge proportions of the rest of the nation's fruits and vegetables.[27]

Like the Chinese in America, Japanese people were denied the basic rights of citizenship, but provided work that enriched others. The first generation of Japanese in the United States (known as the *Issei*) had great hopes that the second generation (*Nisei*) would benefit from their hard work, finding higher education and stronger employment.

Their hopes, however, were dashed in December 1941 when the Japanese bombed Pearl Harbor, setting off a national rage against the Japanese, including those who were American citizens either by birth or naturalization. In 1942 President Franklin Roosevelt issued Executive Order 9066 removing all Japanese people from the American West and ordering them into internment camps throughout the western states. Japanese Americans were first housed in stockyards, fairgrounds, and racetracks, but were eventually relocated to ten different internment camps. All their financial assets were frozen. A massive propaganda campaign targeted them as traitors and "enemy aliens." Not until 1988, during the Reagan administration, did the US government pay sixteen billion dollars in reparations to detainees and their descendants.

With an increasing need for labor, in 1942 the United States recruited Mexican workers through the *bracero program*, a formal agreement between the United States and Mexico. The bracero program permitted Mexican citizens to work in the United States for limited, renewable periods of time. The agreement also prohibited discrimination, a stipulation largely ignored by US growers and the federal government. Over half a million braceros provided labor to US companies under this arrangement.

Mexicans in the bracero program endured poor food, excessive charges for rent, discrimination, and exposure to pesticides, but the program provided growers with a large source of cheap labor. Even after World War II, when US soldiers returned home wanting jobs, the program was kept alive because of the interests of agribusiness. The bracero program brought nearly five million Mexicans to the United States between 1942 and 1964, ending only after protests about their horrific working conditions. Many Mexican Americans today can still trace their roots to this program, recalling horrendous treatment and threats of deportation.[28] Viewed as disposable labor, Mexicans worked in low-wage jobs, were segregated in barrios, and attended segregated schools. They were subjected to many of the same indignities that afflicted Black Americans under Jim Crow segregation.

Mexican Americans organized extensively for protection of their civil rights, as did African Americans. A little-known part of the challenge against racial segregation is that eight years prior to the well-known *Brown v. Board of Education* decision in 1954, a federal court of appeals in California had ruled that the separate schools for Mexican Americans in California were unconstitutional, striking down segregation for children of Mexican, Asian, and Indian descent (in *Mendez v. Westminster*). Thurgood Marshall, the African American attorney who argued the *Brown* case before the Supreme Court and later became the first African American Supreme Court Justice, participated in the *Mendez* case, no doubt influencing his argument in the *Brown* case.[29]

Puerto Rican migration to the mainland is somewhat different than for other groups, primarily because Puerto Ricans are US citizens and thus not immigrants. Puerto Rico became a colony of the United States in 1898 following the Spanish-Cuban-American War. The Jones Act of 1917 then granted US citizenship to Puerto Ricans. Puerto Ricans moved back and forth between the island and the US mainland but in significant numbers only after World War II.

Puerto Ricans were drawn to the jobs that the post–World War II economy provided. By 1950 there were three hundred thousand Puerto Ricans on the mainland, most of them in New York City. By 1970, there were 1.5 million Puerto Ricans on the mainland. Today there are over 4.9 million. Typically employed in low-wage, seasonal jobs, Puerto Ricans have provided much of the work that sustains others.[30]

These related and overlapping, but different, histories show ebbs and flows in the demand for labor—ebbs and flows that track alongside patterns of inclusion and exclusion that mark the nation's racial-ethnic history. The exploitation of labor shapes the evolution of the racial order in America. Moreover, throughout this history, whenever native White workers found themselves economically and socially displaced, racial groups and immigrants become scapegoats for White anxieties—anxieties that actually have their origins in the social and economic structures of society. These brief histories show how the labor of people of color enriched others, at the same time keeping people of color either impoverished or economically marginalized.

THE PAST MEETS THE PRESENT

The history of race in America reverberates daily. It echoes in debates about replacing Confederate monuments. It appears in decisions to rename buildings or schools previously named for slave-owning families. It is central to debates about reparations. Revelations about someone's past racist actions also make us wonder if a simple apology is sufficient for finding racial reconciliation now. We cannot assume the racist practices of the past are over. They linger, meaning that opening opportunities now will not necessarily elevate people of color.

Think of the significance of our racial history this way: Would you think you really understood your good friend if you knew nothing about her past? Isn't it the case that the more you know about your friend's biography, the more you understand what she is like? And if she had a problem now and needed your advice, wouldn't it help to know something about her past experiences? As Michelle Obama has written, "Everyone on earth . . . is carrying around an unseen history."[31] Who we are—as individuals, as communities, and as a society—evolves from what has transpired long before, even before we were born.

The bare outlines of our nation's racial history are somewhat familiar to most people. People know slavery existed and was one of the cruelest parts of our national story. Many have learned of the horrific genocide of Native American people and their forced removal from their homelands. The waves of earlier European immigration are part of the nation's origin story. People recognize old black-and-white images from the Civil Rights Movement, images that show marches, church bombings, or fire hoses being turned on Black demonstrators. On the other hand, most people know very little, if anything, about the historical experiences of diverse Latino groups, nor do many know much about the entry and exclusion of different Asian American groups or specific Native American historical experiences.

What people know about different racial and ethnic groups is also sometimes sketchy—or just learned as a passing reference. Perhaps during Hispanic Heritage Month, schoolchildren might learn something about a Mexican American hero or maybe teachers will introduce young students to Asian American food and music during Asian American Heritage Month. Black History Month will also likely be marked with special activities in schools, noting something special about African American lives. Reverend Martin Luther King's birthday is for some a time of deep spiritual recognition or community service, but for many, it is just another day off from work or school.

These commemorative months are intended to weave the diverse histories of our population into the historical narrative about America. They celebrate our multiracial and multicultural heritage, but they also mark people of color as somehow "different" and out of the ordinary, perhaps implying that they are not *the* national story. This was really highlighted for me some years ago when, while browsing in my campus bookstore, I found one section labeled "special studies." In it were *all* the books on Black history, women's studies, and gay and lesbian studies. I don't recall there being anything there about Latinos or Asian Americans. Special studies! We've moved beyond that now, although these significant publications are still found in separately marked sections in most bookstores I know. Don't get me wrong—I love those sections and want them to be identified, but I also want these studies to be part of the whole curriculum in history, literature, the arts, sciences, and social studies.

Why does knowing the history of people of color matter so much? For one thing, knowing our history defines our national identity, just as knowing your friend's biography defines your understanding of her. More than that, historical narratives also provide people with a sense of pride and belonging—that is, when our histories are included in the overarching narrative. How history is told also reflects the values and beliefs central to any society's culture. History, however, is not just about commemorating the past. It is about understanding the present and guides us in directing the course of change. In the words of William Faulkner, "The past is never dead. It's not even past."[32]

As distant as they may seem, past practices and policies influence the racial inequality that we see today. This does not mean something as direct as that slavery caused today's racial inequality or that annexation of Mexico is the reason for Mexican Americans' current socioeconomic status. Rather, as we have seen, the cumulation of past practices has an ongoing effect, allowing some groups to move forward while others are held back. When you understand racism as an institutional and systemic series of actions and inactions—more than the result of individual prejudice—you learn that racial inequality today is the result of a long history of actions and policies that extend far beyond individual actions and beliefs. In the sobering words of comedian Jon Stewart, the past has "left us with a gaping racial wound that will not heal."[33]

When people look back at the current period, perhaps fifty years from now, maybe one hundred, what will they say about the nation's race relations? Will historians report that our national identity became more inclusive, multiracial, and multicultural? Or will this time be understood as a period of retrenchment—a time when some people's rights were abridged and national identity was narrowly framed on behalf of White people?

How history gets written in the future will depend on what people do now to address racial injustice in our society. What story will be told in years to come? Whose story will it be? Will it be a story of reconciliation and inclusion or will it be a story, like that of the past, of continuing tension and division? We are all familiar with the maxim that if we do not know our history, we are bound to repeat it. As poet and writer Maya Angelou said, "History, despite its wrenching pain, cannot be unlived, but if faced with courage, need not be lived again."[34] What can we do to set such a course? That is the subject of the next chapter.

CHAPTER 6

Getting Smart about Race, Then Doing Something about It

Build bridges, instead of walls.
—ASSOCIATE SUPREME COURT JUSTICE
SONIA SOTOMAYOR[1]

ONE EVENING JUST BEFORE THE CHRISTMAS HOLIDAY, I WAS having dinner with a friend at a local restaurant. Seated next to us was a very large family celebrating the holiday together. Several generations were present. The oldest man, a White man as far as I could tell, was seated at the head of the table. The rest of the family was arrayed by age at the long, rectangular table—older women and other older men near the head of the table; the youngest people at the other end. Five adorable young girls, about age three to six or so, were dressed in their holiday finery and were running around the table throughout the dinner, snuggling up to the woman who seemed to be their grandmother and hugging other adults.

This is a scene probably played out thousands of times in different places, especially during holidays and other family occasions. Family celebrations bring different generations together to recognize cultural traditions. Such celebrations certainly include various family dramas, but also showcase a lot of family love. There was nothing unusual about what I was observing at this holiday table. All but one of the adults was apparently White. The one adult woman of color was not identifiable as from a particular group. If appearance tells us anything, she could have been a mix of Southeast Asian and African American. Two of the youngest girls appeared to be African American and they were being treated with great love and affection.

Scenes such as this give me hope that we can, someday, unite across various differences, despite the racial problems in our society. Families who not that many years ago might have shunned interracial marriage now hug and praise their multiracial kin. In my own family, I am quite sure that our grandmother would be turning in her grave if she knew she now had an African American grandson-in-law and two mixed-race, identifiably Black great-grandchildren. Change has happened even though we have a long way to go toward full and true racial justice.

The greater embrace of interracial relationships shows us that love can bridge the gap that race too often creates. Yet, the greater acceptance of interracial marriage and multiracial people also makes it seem as if race does not matter so much, but it does.

I don't want to be naïve. Interracial marriage, even interracial friendships, is still rare (10 percent of all marriages), but if some people can bridge racial differences in our most intimate relationships, why can we not do so in society more broadly? At the very same time that I can observe a loving mixed-race family sitting so happily together, I can also walk down the streets of any nearby city and see many homeless people, too many of them Black men, begging for money, sleeping over steam vents, and appearing completely dispossessed by the glitzy city around them.

But you don't have to observe such stark contrast to see the reality of race in America, as I hope this book has shown. On any given day in the United States, anyone with a discerning eye can witness the injustices of racial inequality. Acts and statements of racism, anti-Semitism, Islamophobia, and xenophobia (fear of immigrants) have been all too frequent in the national news. As I wrote this book, it seemed there were new examples of group hatred blasted forth in the national news every day, sometimes more than twice a day. And if you are a person of color, you don't have to watch the media to witness racism. It will likely be in your face on a regular basis—a fact I wish more White people would understand.

Still, even with the vast amount of research and writing about racism that shows its systemic nature, most people continue to think of racial inequality as the result of individual attitudes—as if racism would go away if people would only change their minds. This book has asked you to think differently about race and racism. Here's what we know:

First, race is not a biological fact; it is socially created and socially sustained. As a socially produced concept, the idea of race was created with a purpose—to justify the exploitation of groups so defined. When you fully grasp how race is constructed by society, you realize that it will take societal, not just individual, changes to dislodge racism.

Second, racism is rooted in society, but is experienced in immediate, face-to-face experiences—both for people of color and for White people. *Racism hurts* and those wounds can be very deep. Racial wounds, though, do not hurt only individual people. Racial wounds hurt society as a whole. By not utilizing the talents and creativity of all, the nation fails to realize its full potential. Whenever a society robs some of its citizens of their full humanity, all of society is injured.

Third, racial inequality can be neither understood nor changed solely through individual attitudes. Certainly, we need to change individual attitudes and actions, but we also need sweeping societal changes. Changing individual beliefs and behaviors is not a trivial matter, but it will not necessarily change larger forces in society—forces that advantage some and disadvantage others. Of course, it is important to lessen individual prejudices and disrupt racist behavior, but these changes alone do not change racism as an institutional phenomenon. Focusing change only on individual attitudes also runs the risk of making it seem that racism is solely the fault of those with overtly racist views. Such thinking lets otherwise well-meaning people off the hook even when they may be benefiting from racism in society. Reducing racism must be the responsibility of us all.

Fourth, dominant groups develop commonsense, though incorrect, explanations of racism that divert attention from the societal reasons for racial inequality. Many of these explanations blame the victims of racism for their own plight. Blaming the victim deflects attention from the systemic basis of racial inequality and puts the responsibility for change primarily on the very people most hurt by racism. Most people wouldn't say women are responsible for sexism or gay people are to blame for homophobia, so why do people so easily blame people of color and the poor for their own oppression? As long as we blame others for faults that lie in the foundation of society, we only worsen the pain of racism and avoid taking actions that could otherwise improve the lives of so many.

Finally, the advantages and disadvantages that accrue to different racial groups are cumulative. Past actions and policies, along with current behaviors, have produced the social and economic differences we see now. Without recognizing how historical injustices have shaped racial inequality, we might not only reproduce past mistakes, but will overlook the many factors that shape current opportunities for people of color.

These points anchor our understanding of racial inequality in a framework that goes beyond commonsense notions. Getting smart about race means understanding that racism exists at every level—in our attitudes, our actions, our interpersonal relationships, our encounters with different people, and in the very core of our social institutions. Such an understanding means change must come at all of these levels and be anchored in a comprehensive understanding of the multidimensional nature of the nation's racial problems.

THE FULL GAMUT OF RACISM

The recent visibility of white nationalist movements and other demonstrations of white supremacy has made overt racism all too obvious. As we have seen, racism is not, however, just the action of hostile white supremacists. Thinking of racism as only the attitudes and behaviors of White nationalists risks overlooking the other forms that racism takes in society. Racism runs the gamut from individual attitudes to being built into basic social institutions, such as schools, housing, health care, criminal justice, and the economy. In other words, racism is individual, interpersonal, *and* institutional.

At the individual level, subtle forms of racism are present even when people may be barely aware of their own biases. People learn racial attitudes in their families, from their peers, from the media, and from numerous other influences in society. In the absence of any information to the contrary, these attitudes leave people ill-informed about racism and its consequences, particularly if they are not on the receiving end of its ugliness. Learned attitudes can, however, be changed—usually through education. The first appendix of this book provides questions for community groups to explore, hopefully with an eye toward change.

Attitudes are, though, only the most easily observed form of racism. Racism is also an ideology—that is, a whole constellation of beliefs rooted in society that tries to validate the existing status quo. Racist ideology mystifies the real basis of racial inequality—that is, it perpetuates white supremacy. This is why racism is so tricky. You might not actually *be* a white supremacist or think that White people should be the most powerful, but the ideology of racism (that is, a belief in white supremacy) can creep into your commonsense notions, making White people feel, think, and act in ways—conscious or not—that subordinate people of color. The only way to overcome this is to be constantly alert to how one's own behavior and attitudes might be subordinating others.

You might have learned racial ideology in school if your textbooks presented people of color only as exceptions, not part of the main historical narrative. For example, when students learn American history through the lens of dominant groups, people of color are sidelined. Such an approach overlooks how the treatment of different racial and ethnic groups has been central to the making of American institutions. When the histories and contributions of people of color are ignored or minimized in educational curricula, notions of white supremacy are reproduced even if no one consciously says so. Transforming educational curricula to be inclusive of the full range of people's histories, culture, and ideas is then critical to addressing racial inequality—and for fully educating all people about the experiences and contributions of people of color.

The mass media is another way racial ideology is perpetuated. When images of Muslims, Latinos, Native people, African Americans, or any other group are presented in demeaning, threatening, or even comic ways, racial ideology is reproduced. This is why having people of color portrayed in positive and affirming ways is so important. When people see stereotypes in the media, especially if they have little contact with people different from themselves, they can easily come to think of others in limited and insulting ways. And, if people of color never see themselves portrayed in affirming ways, their sense of worth can be diminished. Additionally, racial ideology is expressed through the words and ideas of powerful people in society, whether as national leaders, political pundits, or news commentators. This is why it is so important to have people of color in positions of thought leadership.

The full gamut of racism also includes interpersonal interaction. Our interpersonal encounters are where the day-to-day reality of racial inequality plays out. If you do not question your interactions with people different from you, you are likely to prolong racism. White people seldom recognize how their interaction with people of color can stifle and hurt them. A White person who consistently interrupts Latino colleagues in a meeting or who speaks over African American women during conversations; someone who avoids eye-to-eye contact with Muslim Americans or who expresses doubts that a Black person's experience of racism is true:

These are all ways that racial ideology is played out in everyday social interaction. If questioned, such behaviors can be stopped.

The full gamut of racism includes the fact that racism is built into existing social institutions. Although institutional racism is harder to see than individual racism, its effect is no less consequential. Those consequences are well documented—in income inequality, the gap in educational inequality, the high degree of segregation in society, racial health disparities, and the overrepresentation of people of color in the nation's jails and prisons. Every one of these places is an institutional site where change is needed, but that change must come through institutional reform.

Change can feel overwhelming, but there are things we can do. Even small steps will matter, along with some big ones. Let's start with some ideas.

WHY CAN'T WE ALL GET ALONG? INDIVIDUAL CHANGE

A White friend once told me that, as she has learned more about the history of racial injustice, she feels guilty being White. I suspect this is a common feeling. It is easy for White people to feel ashamed of how people of color have been treated, but shame and guilt are disabling feelings. When my friend said she felt guilty about being White, I suggested she could learn from her growing awareness and then do something about it. Education is a first step. There are various ways people can educate themselves about racism, both formally and informally.

In my case, I grew up as a White person with little understanding about race or racism. Early on, I held numerous racial stereotypes, misconceptions, and was downright ignorant about racism and its effects. My education and exposure to other ways of thinking transformed my thinking and I became committed to teaching and writing about race. As a White person, I had to learn to listen to the experiences of people of color without taking an all-knowing stance. I learned how much I benefit from white privilege and learned to be aware of that while thinking, writing, and talking about race. I know that, because of my white privilege, I can talk about race without people questioning my expertise or thinking I am acting out of self-interest.

As I educated myself about race, I had to question the stereotypes and misconceptions I learned while growing up. I began to see the subtle, and sometimes not so subtle, ways that white supremacy shapes how White people interact with people of color. I benefited enormously from working in mixed-race groups and on behalf of programs designed to promote the success of people of color in school.

The changes for me were not without risk (such as by being embarrassed or ashamed), nor have there not been mistakes along the way. I understand that challenging racism is a lifelong commitment and that I have to repeatedly challenge myself and others to understand race in more liberating ways. Being raised to treat people as I wanted to be treated myself has guided me along the way, as did being taught the core value of fairness. Because I teach students about race, I have had to learn how to identify and speak up against racism while doing so in a way that is challenging but not demeaning or overbearing.

Admittedly, I think most of the change in US race relations must come from White people, although it cannot occur exclusively there. After all, in most situations, White people have the most power—in some cases, significant power—to make a difference. This does not mean that people of color have no such responsibility, but White people should not expect people of color to do most of the work of change. In the now-classic volume aptly titled *This Bridge Called My Back*, Cherríe Moraga writes about how women of color have all too often been walked over as they work for change. She writes, "How can we—this time—not use our bodies to be thrown over a river of tormented history to bridge the gap?"[2] Her words powerfully state the price women of color have too often paid for challenging racism.

Change likely means different things for people of color than for White people. For example, people of color might need to create safe spaces where they can talk about race without fear of insult or attack. Safe spaces in schools and workplaces are where people of color can get support, express anger, and build coalitions without someone telling them they are wrong, "self-segregating," or downright crazy. White people need to understand this, although they typically do not.

I believe that change in race relations fundamentally begins with building empathy. Empathy is not, however, the same thing as pity. Pity assumes domination, as if one is looking down on others and feels sorry for them. Pitying other people makes them seem like objects and not fully human—one of the prerequisites of racist thinking. Empathy, on the other hand, is about finding affinity and common ground with other people. Empathy builds union and commitment, not judgment or superiority.

Where does empathy come from? Empathy might grow from interracial friendships or from working in integrated groups toward a common goal. Unfortunately, the high degree of racial segregation in our society obstructs such opportunities, but you can create opportunities for mixed-race interaction. Doing so purposefully within schools and organizations is one way to foster empathy, but you cannot leave group dynamics to chance or racism will resurface. Those who organize and lead such groups need to ensure that people of color are not silenced or discounted.

People can also build empathy by immersing themselves in the felt worlds of others, perhaps through greater exposure to the writing and artistic works of people from different groups or backgrounds. But White people must be careful not to appropriate the creative works of people of color—a tendency especially common among young people. White youth often claim the accouterments of Latino, Asian, or Black culture (such as dress, lingo, musical taste, and so forth), but without any compassion or real knowledge of Latino, Asian, or Black history. Appropriating culture is then just another form of white privilege—as if one can play at "being Latino," "being Asian," or "acting Black" without any of the penalties from actually being Latino, Asian, or Black.

White people have much to learn about racism, including listening carefully and without judgment, especially when people of color speak. A White person might not understand or agree with what people of color say, but they should not ignore it—or, worse, just assume that it is wrong. It is also important to know that people of color might be angry. Anger can be difficult to confront, but it is not a reason to avoid uncomfortable discussions about race.

Most of all, White people must assume that racism exists because it does. Denying that racism is real or saying it is about something else only undermines and disregards what people of color experience and know.

COLOR-BLIND OR COLOR-CONSCIOUS? THE ONGOING SIGNIFICANCE OF RACE

A friend of mine recently asked me, "Don't you want a color-blind society?" I wanted to say yes, but I couldn't. Actually, I wanted to say, "Yes and no." The question is seemingly simple, but the answer is not. It seems that all but the most die-hard racists share the dream that Dr. Martin Luther King Jr. espoused for his four children when he said he wished that they might "one day live in a nation where they will not be judged by the color of their skin, but by the content of their character."[3] Dr. King's children are now adults, but we have not come near this ideal, nor does it seem we will anytime soon—not even for his grandchildren or his great-grandchildren.

Many Americans embrace the idea of a color-blind society, as do I, but there are limits to what color-blind solutions can do. For people of color, color-blindness might even evoke an angry response—one more hurt in the array of racial wounds. A biracial friend of mine recently told me about his White mother who often declared proudly that she "didn't see color." As her mixed-race (Black and White) son, my friend said his mother's saying so always made him feel invisible—by his own mother, no less! Maybe you will think of him and his pain the next time you hear someone say, "I don't see color. People are all alike!"

To be sure, Dr. King's ideal guides much of our nation's approach to racial justice. A legal framework of equal rights is in place, undergirded by the constitutional principle of equal protection, as established in 1865 by the Fourteenth Amendment to the US Constitution. Dr. King's exhortation, given at a time of racial crisis in American history, appealed then, as it does now, to the moral conscience of Americans to live up to the American ideal of equal justice for all. History has shown, however, that color-blind actions do not in and of themselves dismantle the entrenched system of racial inequality. Despite the appeal of King's call, a fundamental question remains: Should we use color-blind approaches to achieve racial equality or do we need race-conscious actions to eliminate racial injustice?

It is one thing to be color-blind by not judging people based on their racial or ethnic identity, but it is quite another thing to deny the significance of race in people's life experiences. When color-blind actions overlook the ongoing significance of race, they can reproduce existing forms of inequality, possibly even create more harm. Here's an example: Shutting down shops, markets, or banks in minority neighborhoods because they are not profitable might make good business sense, but it reduces needed community services. Such color-blind action, even in the absence of race-specific intent, only results in more racial disadvantage.

Reasonable people may disagree about race-conscious solutions, but they are sometimes necessary to open opportunities to people otherwise excluded. For example, most people believe that employment and educational decisions should be based solely on merit. But ask yourself: Can you objectively measure merit when all of a person's prior experience was nestled in inequality?

Most people believe, for example, that college admissions should be based on objective measures, such as students' grades and performance on standardized exams. Yet grades and standardized test scores can be riddled with bias—such as the quality of a student's previous school, the content of the school curriculum, familiarity with test content, the cultural bias of test questions, even the bias of test examiners. These factors all influence something so seemingly "objective" as a grade point average or a test score.

So, should race matter in college admissions? So far, the US Supreme Court has said yes—to a degree. Race can matter as long as there are not "set asides" or quotas for students of color. In other words, the Supreme Court has ruled that race can be considered along with other factors. The logic comes from social science evidence showing that *all* students learn more in diverse environments.[4] When states have disallowed the use of race, such as by eliminating affirmative action programs, the result has been a significant drop in the number of students of color enrolled.

Yet the public has little appetite for race-based decisions—in part because race has been used so perniciously in the nation's past. Three-quarters of the public (73 percent) say colleges should not take race into account. Even more (81 percent) say gender should not be a factor; 57 percent say athletic ability should not be taken into account.[5] This may be because so many people believe that there is equal opportunity in society—a belief contradicted by reams of sound social science research.

Of course, no one wants to be excluded from a school or a job based on their race—or any other characteristic, for that matter. The color-blind ideal resonates with the American belief in individualism and personal merit—that is, the idea that people should be judged and treated based on their own actions, not on their personal identity, whether that is race, ethnicity, class, gender, disability, or anything else. But as long as racial inequality results from the cumulative effects of the past, actions for change must sometimes consider race as part of the strategy.

Being race-conscious means taking into account *all* the factors that have led us to this point and developing comprehensive policies to address them all. Even with laws in place that guarantee equal rights, racial inequality remains deeply entrenched in US institutions. Consequently, race-conscious changes are needed in order to open doors for previously excluded groups. As former Supreme Court Justice Harry Blackmun once said, "In order to get beyond racism, we must first take account of race. There is no other way. And in order to treat some persons equally, we must treat them differently."[6]

CHANGING RESISTANT INSTITUTIONS

Changing institutions is harder than changing individual attitudes and action, but change can happen, as history shows. Many programs and policies have been effective in reducing racial inequality, not least of which are civil rights laws that have opened educational, employment, and political opportunities for countless people of color. Anti-poverty programs during the 1960s also made a huge difference in lowering the earlier high rates of poverty among African Americans. These historic achievements tell us that a commitment from the federal government to reduce racial inequality can truly matter. The question is whether we will commit to doing so now.

Much of the time, change within institutions is stimulated by external forces, especially social movements and the mobilization of people who demand change. Other external forces can also produce change at the national level. Population change can bring more diverse voices to the dialogue around race; changes in political leadership can change the national agenda; demands by religious leaders that we live up to our national values of equality and justice can tweak the nation's conscience and spark further change: These and other external forces have transformed even the most seemingly tenacious institutions.

Change does not, however, typically come from the top, one reason people are so cynical about the effectiveness of elected officials. Rather, change usually comes from people who stand up to address an issue affecting their daily life. For example, Alicia Garza, Patrice Cullers, and Opal Tometi, who were working as community organizers, were outraged when George Zimmerman shot and killed Trayvon Martin. Alicia Garza posted a letter on Facebook expressing her love of Black people, saying, "Our Lives Matter, Black Lives Matter." The three of them then founded the #BlackLivesMatter movement, first as an online community. Quickly, though, #BlackLivesMatter became a national campaign to protest police violence against Black people.

There are countless examples of such activism—activism sparked when someone sees a need that spurs them to work for social justice. In another example, Ai-Jen Poo began her activist work as an undergraduate student volunteering in a battered women's shelter. With the skills she learned as a volunteer, she began organizing domestic workers in New York City, namely immigrants with little ability to navigate the legal system. Ultimately, Ai-Jen Poo created and now directs the National Domestic Workers' Alliance, an organization promoting the rights of domestic workers—the vast majority of whom are women of color.

These are examples of people working for change who ended up on the national stage. Other times, people work more locally. Either way, change begins when ordinary people decide to do something about an issue that touches their everyday life. Activism might mean working in a workplace, school, or other organization to develop policies and programs that address racial injustice. Sometimes, activism involves public demonstration—boycotts, marches, sit-ins, or other such projects. The point is that change begins at the personal level—seeing a problem, understanding its origin, deciding to do something about it, figuring out who can work with you, developing a plan for action, and then taking action.

Change might mean working in an existing group (large or small) or it might mean creating something new. Change can come from within institutions, such as lobbying to pass laws or create policies designed to open doors, reduce discrimination, and promote opportunities in educational or work organizations. Anti-racism training, mentoring programs, and leadership education are examples of how organizations can promote opportunities for people of color, while raising the awareness of White people.

Because the problem of racial inequality is so vast, approaches large and small and within and outside of existing institutions are needed. The historical record teaches us that the comprehensive struggle for racial justice involves multiple groups who take different approaches to effect change. People organize for change, using whatever resources they can to advocate for their rights, as was the case in the Civil Rights Movement. African American people organized boycotts, sit-ins, marches, and countless other actions to demand their rights. Their efforts, like those of people in other racial justice movements, are an inspiration to those who now feel that the magnitude of change is daunting.

Reducing racial inequality will require efforts on multiple fronts, not least of which is grappling with the growing inequality of our time. Although the income and wealth gaps are especially detrimental for people of color, many people would benefit from policies to reduce income and wealth inequality and addressing this vast inequality could give such a movement wide appeal. The high rates of poverty and unemployment among people of color also show the continuing need for anti-poverty and job training programs, including training that would provide the skills necessary in today's advanced technological economy. The nation desperately needs a sound national immigration policy, and clearly there is a need for programs to tackle the different dimensions of racial inequality, including investment in housing, education, and criminal justice reform.

Because the need for change is so great, a comprehensive plan is necessary. This will take commitment from national leaders and a groundswell of public support—a national call to action. That call, like those of the past, will need to recognize the significance of race in every aspect of our lives and at all levels of society.

Racism is not likely to go away in our lifetimes. Changing individual attitudes and actions is a good first step, as is having serious conversations about race. Individual change, though, is not enough. Systemic problems require systemic solutions. Institutional change must be part of the agenda.

WILL RACISM FADE AWAY?

For a very long time, racism in the United States was defined as a "black-white" divide. As W. E. B. Du Bois notably wrote in 1903, "The problem of the twentieth century is the problem of the color line."[7] We are now well into the twenty-first century and the color line, though blurred, is still with us. It has, however, morphed into something more like a rainbow of many different groups.

Population data confirm that the United States is becoming more racially and ethnically diverse. Until recently, African Americans were the largest so-called minority group. Latinos now surpass African Americans as the largest "minority." Population projections also predict that Asian Americans and Latinos will outgrow both Whites and African Americans in the years to come. As a result, the White, non-Hispanic population, as a proportion of the total US population, is expected to decline—to 44 percent of the population by 2050.

Immigration, racial intermarriage, an increase in those identifying as multiracial, and the higher birth rate among some minority populations mean that the black-white divide that historically defined race in the United States is no longer as sharp as it once seemed to be. As society becomes more multiracial, will racism fade away? Or will the color line just become a more colorful bar? Even a rainbow seems to have bars between its different hues.

Some think that demographic changes will blur racial boundaries, lessening the threat of racial prejudice and hate. Yet dreams that society was becoming "post-racial" now seem an illusion—an illusion shattered by the recent rise in hate crimes and racist white nationalist actions. White supremacist violence has shaken the belief that we have somehow moved beyond race. On the other hand, the public has also awakened to the obstinate reality of racism, anti-Semitism, and other forms of group hatred. Once again, we seem to be at a fork in the road toward racial justice. Will the nation choose the path toward racial reconciliation or will we settle for the status quo?

In the face of the antagonisms now dividing the nation, it is difficult to imagine the diminishment of racial hostilities. In fact, the opposite could happen. As the society becomes more multiracial and Whites become a smaller proportion of the population, too many White people feel that their place in society is under threat. Some desire a return to an old racial order, even though they may not overtly say so. They then target old scapegoats, as if people of color, and immigrants, too, not society itself, are the basis for their fragile status.

There are, however, signs of hope. Especially if you take a long-range view, you can see progress toward greater racial equity. The number of African Americans and Latinos who are middle class has grown. Younger generations are more racially tolerant than older generations. Younger people also tend to see racial and ethnic diversity as a good thing for society.[8] There are more Latino, Black, Muslim, Native, and Asian people in visible positions of leadership and power. Politicians now also have to be mindful of the needs and interests of people of color because of their potential influence in elections. Laws are in place that, at least in principle, protect the rights of minorities.

With every sign of progress, however, there are cautions. The Black and Latino hold on the middle class is fragile. Both groups lag behind the White middle class in economic status. Whether young people's attitudes will hold as they grow older and as society evolves remains to be seen. Voting rights are being abridged. Protecting voting rights is a critical element of change. The backlash against Muslims elected to national office has been vicious and deeply disturbing. None of the gains made can be taken for granted, and racial progress does not necessarily follow a linear line toward greater equality. Progress made can be all too easily taken away. On the road to racial justice there will be ups and downs.

As I was writing this book, an image kept popping into my head—that of a teeter-totter: A teeter-totter, or seesaw, is a balanced board found on children's playgrounds. Each child sits on one end of the board, which is balanced on a fulcrum. If one child is heavier than the other and does not sit in just the right place, the lighter-weight child stays up in the air and the heavier child stays on the ground. The trick is to balance the weight by where each child sits. Should the child on the bottom jump off, the other child will come crashing down.

This image suggests that our nation has teetered between the countervailing forces of the heavy weight of racism and the uplifting struggle for racial justice. Which one will outweigh the other? Where will you sit in this struggle? It seems that the weight of racism keeps us stuck in the muck of racial inequality, but with a national call to action, we could keep from falling further and potentially even elevate our nation to greater heights.

AN AMERICAN CONVERSATION AND A COMMITMENT TO ACTION

It may be naïve to take an optimistic view of the possibilities for change, but hope and action are essential. Change has happened before, and more is possible. Over the course of history, the long march to racial justice has come through the actions and leadership of ordinary people, some of whom rose to prominence; others worked more quietly, but diligently, on the ground, organizing what has been a revolution in the nature of racial inequality—but an incomplete one.[9]

Will American people have the will, both individually and collectively, to continue the important work of change? Among many pockets of the population, there is a clear desire to do something about racial inequality. And there are many signs that people want a more just and fair nation. We just do not always know how. Ignoring racial troubles, however, is not the answer.

The history of anti-racist work shows that change does not come from above, although clearly the support of national leaders is critical. Change comes from the efforts of people who challenge existing practices and social institutions and who use education and a change in consciousness to achieve their goals. This means we need an alliance, no matter how fragile, between White people and people of color. Creating such an alliance will require White people to get smart about race—developing knowledge and empathy to enable them to be good allies and agents of change. Although the possibility for change may seem overwhelming, there is plenty you can do. In your case, what will that be?

Appendix A

Finding Common Ground: Questions for Conversation

Important Things to Consider

As important as it is that we do so, talking about race can be difficult—for various reasons and in different ways for different people. When holding such critical conversations, it is important for group facilitators to guide such conversations with an awareness of how easily people of color can be silenced, dismissed, and/or disputed. At the same time, facilitators should understand that some White people are reluctant to speak about race at all.

Because race will affect group interaction, it is important to establish ground rules for the discussion. If there is time, the group should discuss and agree to ground rules before discussion begins. Facilitators can then remind people of these guidelines should the conversation require such an intervention (such as when someone talks too much, when someone disputes another person's reality, if someone is reluctant to speak, or other such actions). Because people are usually unaware of how much they talk, it can be useful to use a timer to ensure that everyone has a fair chance to participate.

The following questions might be useful to facilitators as a way of guiding the conversation:

"I can see why you might think that, but have you considered . . . ?"

"That is a common reaction; has anyone else felt the same way/heard the same thing?"

"How do you suppose someone experiencing [fill in the blank] might feel?"

"How might that be similar to (or different from) the experience of ____?" [fill in the blank]

"I can understand why someone would think that, but have you considered where that idea comes from?"

"Experiencing racism is exhausting [or use another word, depending on what you hear]. I can hear that in your voice. Is there something the group can do for you?"

The following web pages have excellent suggestions for using and developing ground rules and for leading group discussions on race and racism:

- http://www.edchange.org/multicultural/activities/groundrules.html
- https://sites.google.com/site/communityconversationstraining/ground-rules
- https://ct.counseling.org/2015/12/race-talk-and-facilitating-difficult-racial-dialogues
- https://docplayer.net/21844170-Ten-tips-for-facilitating-classroom-discussions-on-sensitive-topics.html

QUESTIONS FOR GROUP DISCUSSION

Chapter 1: Race: A Thoroughly Social Idea

1. What would you say to someone who declared, "We are all just human beings. Race doesn't matter anymore."
2. Some think that people should not be asked to indicate their race on the many and various forms where this question is asked. Do you agree or disagree? Why?
3. Go to the Public Broadcasting Service (PBS) website for the film *Race: The Power of an Illusion.* Do the "Sorting People" exercise (http://www.pbs.org/race/002_SortingPeople/002_00-home

.htm). After tallying how many you (and others, if doing this in a group) got right, discuss what you looked for to identify people and whether these are good indicators of "race." How does this exercise illustrate that race is a social construction?

Chapter 2: Feeling Race in Everyday Life

1. Think about the opening vignette about the handknit scarf. What would your reaction have been had it been your scarf that was taken? What is the significance of race in this event? Would you react differently to this experience had the owner of the scarf been White?

2. Identify a situation where you have witnessed or experienced a racial insult. How might you have intervened in this situation? Would there be different consequences from such an intervention, depending on your racial identity?

3. When discussing topics where there are strong feelings, it is often difficult to be persuasive with facts. When confronting racism, how might people use emotion to appeal to anti-racist education? What are the risks, challenges, and benefits of doing so?

Chapter 3: Who, Me? I'm Not a Racist, But ...

1. What do you think it means to say that prejudiced people are not the only racists in the United States?

2. How can we recognize racial, ethnic, and cultural differences without stumbling into racism?

3. You have just heard someone make a racist statement. What might you say?

Chapter 4: What Did You Say? Contesting Commonsense Racism

1. What would you say now to someone who said, "If people would just try harder, poverty would not be such a problem for people of color"?

2. What specific forms of support have you received (or not) to be in the position you are now? How has your understanding of such support changed based on your reading of this chapter?

3. Ask members of the group to describe any immigration experiences that are part of their family background. What specific conditions affected this immigration experience? How do these experiences relate to contemporary immigration issues?

Chapter 5: But That Was Then—I Didn't Have Anything to Do with It

1. What common experiences have different racial and ethnic groups shared over the course of American history? How do they differ?

2. Had we not engaged in the racist practices of the past (such as redlining, racial covenants, and other impediments to social mobility for people of color), how might things be different now?

3. How do you think the history of the current period will be written fifty years from now?

Chapter 6: Getting Smart about Race, Then Doing Something about It

1. If you could do just one thing to reduce racial inequality in the United States, what would it be?

2. Name a social policy currently under consideration at the federal or local level. What is the likely impact of this policy on people of color?

3. Many people think of anti-racist activists in stereotypical ways, but activism comes in many forms. In what specific ways might you think of yourself as an anti-racist activist?

Appendix B

Further Resources

Readers who want to learn more about race and racism will find the following books, films, and videos especially useful. These resources could be used for community-based discussions, workshops in various organizations, and book clubs.

In addition to the resources below, readers who want more documentation and detail about the subject matter of this book can consult Margaret L. Andersen, *Race in Society: The Enduring American Dilemma* (Lanham, MD: Rowman & Littlefield, 2017), a book written primarily for college student learning.

CHAPTER 1: RACE: A THOROUGHLY SOCIAL IDEA

Books

George M. Fredrickson, *Racism: A Short History* (Princeton, NJ: Princeton University Press, 2015). Comprehensive (though brief) review of how the linked ideas of race and racism have developed in the United States, South Africa, and Nazi Germany.

Laura Gomez, *Manifest Destinies: The Making of the Mexican American Race* (New York: New York University Press, 2018). Details how Mexican Americans came to be seen as second-class citizens, focusing on how they were racialized by their treatment in the United States.

Joseph Graves, *The Race Myth: Why We Pretend Race Exists in America* (New York: Dutton, 2004). Debunks the idea that race is rooted in human biological differences and links the idea of race to racist social institutions.

Dorothy Roberts, *Fatal Invention: How Science, Politics, and Big Business Re-Create Race in the Twenty-First Century* (New York: New Press, 2011). Documents the role of major social institutions in creating the concept of race.

Lori L. Tharp, *Same Family, Different Colors: Confronting Colorism in America's Diverse Families* (Boston: Beacon, 2016). Contemporary analysis of how colorism—that is, the ranking of people by skin color, emerges in society.

Film/Video

Great Is Their Sin: Biological Determinism in an Age of Genomics (52 mins.) https://www.youtube.com/watch?v=idrVWkXsWpQ; brief version (17 minutes) at https://www.youtube.com/watch?v=xO-4e0ZLoU8. A lecture by biological scientist Dr. Joseph Graves presents the latest genetic science developments showing how race is a social construction. Easily accessible to a general audience.

Race: The Power of an Illusion: The Difference Between Us, Part 1 (San Francisco: California Newsreel, 2003; 56 mins.). Part 1 of this three-part documentary shows that, despite beliefs to the contrary, human beings do not fall into distinct biological groups. The film shows how myths about race have developed over the years and illustrates in clear terms how DNA evidence contradicts constructed beliefs about supposed racial difference.

Race: The Power of An Illusion: The Story We Tell, Part 2 (San Francisco: California Newsreel, 2003; 56 mins.). Part 2 of this three-part documentary series shows how beliefs about race have developed over the course of history. Ideas about racial inferiority have tracked alongside the development of the United States.

CHAPTER 2: FEELING RACE IN EVERYDAY LIFE

Books

Margaret L. Andersen and Patricia Hill Collins, eds., *Race, Class, and Gender: Intersections and Inequalities* (Boston: Cengage, 2020). A popular collection of essays exploring how race, class, *and* gender together influence diverse experiences of inequality.

Elijah Anderson, *The Cosmopolitan Canopy: Race and Civility in Everyday Life* (New York: W. W. Norton, 2011). Explores how people can live in urban environments with racial civility, despite the tensions that racism produces.

Ta-Nehisi Coates, *Between the World and Me* (New York: Spiegel & Grau, 2015). Writing a letter to his adolescent son, Coates powerfully shows the burden of racism and its exploitation of Black people.

Film/Video

The Color of Fear (Oakland, CA: Stirfry Seminars and Consulting, 1994; 90 mins.). Powerful documentary based on conversation between eight men of different racial-ethnic backgrounds that explores the anguish that racism has created. Can be broken into smaller segments for viewing and discussion.

The Latino List (New York: Filmmakers Library, 2011; Volume 1, 57 mins.; Volume 2, 49 mins.). Produced by HBO, this two-volume set includes interviews with prominent Latinos. In Volume 1, accomplished people in diverse professions discuss their childhood experiences, how they achieved success, and their continuing challenges. Volume 2 also highlights first-person vignettes by prominent Latinos discussing issues of the day, including immigration and cultural identity.

CHAPTER 3: WHO, ME? I'M NOT A RACIST, BUT . . .

Books

Carol Anderson, *White Rage: The Unspoken Truth of Our Racial Divide* (New York: Bloomsbury, 2016). Anderson argues that social and economic progress for African Americans has consistently been met by opposition, typically under the guise of attitudes and expressions of belief that are based in underlying White anger.

Eduardo Bonilla Silva, *Racism without Racists: Color-Blind Racism and the Persistence of Racial Inequality in America*, 4th ed. (Lanham, MD: Rowman & Littlefield, 2013). Detailed examination of White racial attitudes that are cloaked in color-blind claims even while rooted in the defense of white privilege.

Robin Diangelo, *White Fragility: Why It's So Hard for White People to Talk about Racism* (Boston: Beacon, 2018). Based on what she has heard during anti-racism workshops, Diangelo documents white resistance expressed through various defensive beliefs that show white resistance to racial equity.

Jennifer Eberhardt, *Biased: Uncovering the Hidden Prejudice That Shapes What We See, Think, and Do* (New York: Viking, 2019). Shows how unconscious attitudes affect people's perceptions and behavior. Eberhardt's purpose is to show how revealing such underlying beliefs can reduce racial mistreatment.

Claude Steele, *Whistling Vivaldi: And Other Clues to How Stereotypes Affect Us* (New York: W. W. Norton, 2010). Tracing the development of the concept of stereotype threat, Steele shows how racial perceptions affect people's performance—both in education and in interpersonal relationships.

Beverly Daniel Tatum, *Why Are All the Black Kids Sitting Together in the Cafeteria: And Other Conversations about Race*, 20th anniversary ed. (New York: Basic, 2017). Explores racial identity development for young Black people and situates the need for strong peer connections when people have to live in the context of racism. Her straightforward and clear analysis debunks many of the myths about young people, schools, and cultural racism.

Film/Video

Cracking the Codes: The System of Racial Inequity (Oakland, CA: World Trust Educational Services, Inc. 2012; 75 mins.) https://world-trust.org/product

/cracking-codes-system-racial-inequity. Anti-racism training film shows the causes and consequences of racial beliefs. Discussion guide available.

Mirrors of Privilege: Making Whiteness Visible (Oakland, CA: World Trust Educational Services, 2006); https://world-trust.org/mirrors-of-privilege -making-whiteness-visible. Featuring a number of anti-racist authors and activists, the film portrays the different reactions of White people (including denial, fear, and guilt, among others) as they work to address racial injustice. There is a conversation guide available for group discussion.

White Like Me (San Francisco: Media Education Foundation, 2013, 69 mins.) Author and anti-racist educator Tim Wise discusses race and racism in the United States through the lens of whiteness and white privilege.

CHAPTER 4: WHAT DID YOU SAY? CONTESTING COMMON-SENSE RACISM

Books

Michelle Alexander, *The New Jim Crow: Mass Incarceration in the Age of Colorblindness* (New York: New Press, 2010). Challenging the idea of color-blindness, Alexander examines the detrimental impact on Black communities of the mass incarceration of Black people.

Susan Greenbaum, *Blaming the Poor: The Long Shadow of the Moynihan Report on Cruel Images about Poverty* (New Brunswick, NJ: Rutgers University Press, 2015). Details the causes and consequences of victim blaming and shows its impact on social policies.

Nazli Kibria, Cara Bowman, and Megan O'Leary, *Race and Immigration* (New York: Polity, 2014). In a brief and accessible way examines how immigration shapes racial inequality. Also provides an excellent overview of immigrant labor, historical immigration policies, and immigrant identities.

Thomas M. Shapiro, *Toxic Inequality: How America's Wealth Gap Destroys Mobility, Deepens Racial Inequality, and Threatens Our Future* (New York: Basic, 2017). Discussion of the racial wealth gap and how it threatens core American principles of social mobility, equality, and social justice.

Nicole Gonzalez Van Cleve, *Crook County: Racism and Injustice in America's Largest Criminal Court* (Stanford, CA: Stanford Law Books, 2016). Shows how the justice system reproduces racism even when powerful people in the courtroom are committed to the ideal of color-blindness.

Film/Video

A Day without a Mexican (Santa Monica, CA: Xenon Pictures, 2004; 98 mins.). Satirical film that shows what happens when all the Mexicans in California disappear. Although satire, it shows the impact of Mexicans on the economy.

Latinos Beyond Reel: Challenging a Media Stereotype (San Francisco: Media Education Foundation, 2014; 85 mins.). Documentary showing how the US media portrays Latinos; film challenges viewers to see the impact of these stereotypes and envision other possibilities.

Reel Bad Arabs: How Hollywood Vilifies a People (San Francisco: Media Education Foundation, 2014). Details how stereotypes of Asian people have populated popular culture, from the earliest days of silent movies through contemporary films. The documentary inspires critical thinking about the impact of these persistent images and narratives.

The Return of Navaho Boy (Berkeley, CA: Extension Center for Media and Independent Learning, 2000; 57 mins.). A remake of an old film; the current version shows the impact of uranium exposure on the health of the Navaho nation.

Slaying the Dragon Reloaded (New York: Women Make Movies, 2011; 88 mins.). Shows how Asian women are depicted in US films, noting as well the impact of globalization on how Asian culture is depicted.

CHAPTER 5: BUT THAT WAS THEN—I DIDN'T HAVE ANYTHING TO DO WITH IT

Books

Gordon H. Chang, *Ghosts of Gold Mountain: The Epic Story of the Chinese Who Built the Transcontinental Railroad* (Boston: Houghton Mifflin Harcourt, 2019). In-depth analysis of the extraordinary labor of Chinese workers in building the transcontinental railroad. With compassion and impeccable research, Chang shows the humanity of these workers who labored under inhumane conditions.

Jacqueline Jones, *A Dreadful Deceit: The Myth of Race from the Colonial Era to Obama's America* (New York: Basic, 2013). Drawing from individual lives of African Americans, Jones shows how the concept of race evolves over the course of American history.

Richard Rothstein, *The Color of Law: A Forgotten History of How Our Government Segregated America* (New York: Liveright, 2017). Details the impact of government policies that have produced racial segregation and inequality.

Ronald Takaki, *A Different Mirror: A History of Multicultural America* (Boston: Little, Brown, 1993). Brief but thorough presentation of the histories of diverse racial-ethnic groups, thus providing a more complete view of US history.

Film/Video

Race: The Power of an Illusion: The House We Live In, Part 3 (San Francisco: California Newsreel, 2003; 56 mins.). Details the historical development of US policies that have created the income and wealth inequality we still witness today.

Segregated by Design (Silkworm Studio, 2019; 18 mins.) www.segregated-bydesign.com. Brief video based on the book *The Color of Law*, showing how US governmental policies have created segregation now.

The African Americans: Many Rivers to Cross (Arlington, VA: PBS Distribution, 2013; 360 mins., can be shown in smaller segments). Produced by Henry Louis Gates, focuses on the development of African American culture, political institutions, and identity, even in the face of insurmountable odds.

CHAPTER 6: GETTING SMART ABOUT RACE, THEN DOING SOMETHING ABOUT IT

Books

Crystal Fleming, *How Not to Be Stupid about Race: On Racism, White Supremacy, and the Racial Divide* (New York: Beacon, 2018). Frank presentation of many misconceptions about race, drawing also on the author's experience as a Black queer professor. Challenges commonsense notions of race and racism.

Ibram X. Kendi, *How to Be an Antiracist* (London: Oneworld, 2019). Based on personal experience, Kendi asks people to think about what an anti-racist world would look like and what we must do to move in that direction.

Ed Morales, *Latinx: The New Force in American Politics and Culture* (Brooklyn, NY: Verso, 2018). Details the impact of the growing presence of Latinx people in the US political and social landscape.

Ijeoma Oluo, *So You Want to Talk about Race* (Berkeley, CA: Seal Press, 2018). Describes how race and racism infiltrate every aspect of everyday life and provides guidance for having difficult conversations about race.

Sonia Sotomayor, *My Beloved World* (New York: Knopf, 2013). Autobiographical account of growing up in a strong Puerto Rican family and community—her anchor for later experiences in elite educational institutions and, ultimately, the US Supreme Court.

Dorothy M. Steele and Becki Cohn-Vargas, *Identity Safe Classrooms: Places to Belong and Learn* (Thousand Oaks, CA: Corwin, 2013). Practical suggestions for creating educational settings where all students feel welcome and appreciated.

Film/Video

Eyes on the Prize: America's Civil Rights Years, 1954–1965. Produced by Blackside for PBS (Arlington, VA: PBS Distribution, 2006; 60 mins. per segment). Award-winning fourteen-part series documenting the history of the civil rights movement.

Chicano! History of the Mexican American Civil Rights Movement (Los Angeles: NLCC Educational Media, 1996; 60 mins. per episode). Four-part documentary from PBS documenting the emergence of the Chicano movement.

Symbols of Resistance: A Tribute to the Martyrs of the Chican@ Movement (MVD Entertainment Group, 2017; 72 mins.). Examines student activism, police repression, and issues of Chicano identity as revealed through stories of Chicano activism.

Vincent Who? (San Francisco: Kanopy Streaming, 2016; 41 mins.). Shows the development of Pan-Asian identity in the aftermath of the killing of Vincent Chin by laid-off automobile workers. Also provides a narrative of Asian American history.

Notes

Introduction

1. Joe Biden, *Promise Me, Dad: A Year of Hope, Hardship, and Courage* (New York: Flatiron, 2017), 39.
2. Cameron McWhirter, *Red Summer: The Summer of 1919 and the Awakening of Black America* (New York: Henry Holt, 2011); William D. Carrigan and Clive Webb, "The Lynching of Persons of Mexican Origin or Descent in the United States, 1848–1928," *Journal of Social History* 37 (Winter 2003): 411–38; Paula Giddings, *A Sword among Lions: Ida B. Wells and the Campaign against Lynching* (New York: Amistad, 2008).
3. Abraham Lincoln, "Speech on the Dred Scott Decision," June 26, 1857.

Chapter 1: Race: A Thoroughly Social Idea

1. Rubén Rumbaut, "The Pigments of Our Imagination: The Racialization of the Hispanic-Latino Category," Migration Policy Institute, April 11, 2011, https://www.migrationpolicy.org/article/pigments-our-imagination-racialization-hispanic-latino-category.
2. Jonathan Marks, *Is Science Racist?* (New York: Polity, 2017).
3. Siddhartha Mukherjee, *The Gene: An Intimate History* (New York: Scribner, 2016), 341.
4. C. Matthew Snipp, "Defining Race and Ethnicity: The Constitution, the Supreme Court, and the Census," in *Doing Race: 21 Essays for the Twenty-First Century*, ed. Paula M. Moya and Hazel Rose Marcus (New York: Oxford University Press, 2010), 105–22.
5. Snipp, "Defining Race and Ethnicity."
6. Eduardo Bonilla-Silva, "We Are All Americans! The Latin Americanization of Racial Stratification in the USA," *Race & Society* 5 (2002): 3–16.
7. William I. Thomas, *The Unadjusted Girl* (Boston: Little, Brown, 1931).

Chapter 2: Feeling Race in Everyday Life

1. Jon Stewart, *The Daily Show*, August 26, 2014, http://www.cc.com/video-clips/ufqeuz/the-daily-show-with-jon-stewart-race-off.
2. Lee Mun Wah, *The Color of Fear* (Berkeley, CA: Stir Fry Productions, 1994).
3. John Blake, "Why El Paso and Other Recent Attacks in the US Are Modern Day Lynchings," CNN, https://www.cnn.com/2019/08/17/us/lynchings-racism-new-era-blake/index.html; Carol Anderson, *White Rage: The Unspoken Truth of Our Racial Divide* (New York: Bloomsbury, 2016).

4. Derald Wing Sue, *Microaggressions in Everyday Life: Race, Gender, and Sexual Orientation* (Hoboken, NJ: Wiley, 2010).

5. Adapted from Peggy McIntosh, "White Privilege and Male Privilege: A Personal Account of Coming to See Correspondences through Work in Women's Studies." Working Paper 189, Wellesley Centers for Women, 1983.

6. Diane Goodman, *The Cost of Racism to White People and Why They Should Care about Racial Justice* (Northampton, MA: Focusing Initiatives International, 2017), accessed May 14, 2019, https://focusinginternational.org/the-cost-of -racism-to-white-people-and-why-they-should-care-about-racial-justice.

7. George Lipsitz, *How Racism Takes Place* (Philadelphia: Temple University Press, 2011), 6.

8. Reynolds Farley, Howard Schuman, Suzanne Bianchi, Diane Colasanto, and Shirley Hatchett, "'Chocolate City, Vanilla Suburbs': Will the Trend Toward Racially Separate Communities Continue?" *Social Science Research* 7, no. 4 (1978): 319–44.

9. Daniel T. Lichter, Domenico Parisi, and Michael C. Taquino, "Toward a New Macro-Segregation? Decomposing Segregation Within and Between Metropolitan Cities and Suburbs," *American Sociological Review* 80, no. 4 (2015): 843–73; John Logan and Brian J. Stults, "The Persistence of Segregation in the Metropolis: New Findings from the 2010 Census," Census Brief prepared for Project US2010, 2011, http://www.s4.brown.edu/us2010; Jacob S. Rugh and Douglas S. Massey, "Segregation in Post-Civil Rights America," *Du Bois Review: Social Science Research on Race* 11, no. 2 (2014): 205–32; Sean F. Reardon and Ann Owens, "60 Years after *Brown*: Trends and Consequences of School Segregation," *Annual Review of Sociology* 40 (July 2014): 199–218.

10. Lipsitz, *How Racism Takes Place*, 6.

11. Jason P. Block, Richard A. Scribner, and Karen B. DeSalvo, "Fast Food, Race/Ethnicity, and Income: A Geographic Analysis," *American Journal of Preventive Medicine* 27, no. 3 (2004): 211–17; Carolyn C. Cannuscio, Amy Hillier, Allison Karpyn, and Karen Glanz, "The Social Dynamics of Healthy Food Shopping and Store Choice in an Urban Environment," *Social Science & Medicine* 122 (December 2014): 13–20; Renee E. Walker, Christopher R. Keane, and Jessica G. Burke, "Disparities and Access to Healthy Food in the United States: A Review of Food Deserts Literature," *Health & Place* 16, no. 5 (2010): 876–84.

12. Sofia Kluch, *Low Income Non-Whites in the U.S. Feel as Safe as Nicaraguans* (Princeton, NJ: Gallup Organization, 2018), accessed May 14, 2019, https:// news.gallup.com/opinion/gallup/236969/low-income-nonwhites-feel -safe-nicaraguans.aspx.

13. Meghan A. Rich, "'It Depends on How You Define Integrated': Neighborhood Boundaries and Racial Integration in a Baltimore Neighborhood," *Sociological Forum* 24, no. 4 (2009): 828–53.

14. Gary Orfield, "Housing Segregation Produces Unequal Schools: Causes and Solutions," in *Closing the Opportunity Gap: What America Must Do to Give Every*

Child an Even Chance, ed. Prudence L. Carter and Kevin G. Welner (New York: Oxford University Press, 2013), 40–60.

15. Elijah Anderson, "The White Space," *Sociology of Race & Ethnicity* 1 (January 2015): 10–21.

16. Beverly Daniel Tatum, *Why Are All the Black Kids Sitting Together in the Cafeteria? and Other Conversations about Race* (New York: Basic, 1997), 6.

17. Tatum, *Why Are All the Black Kids Sitting Together?*, 6.

18. Patricia Hill Collins, *Black Feminist Thought: Knowledge, Consciousness, and the Politics of Empowerment* (Boston: Unwin and Hyman, 1990).

19. Joe R. Feagin, *The White Racial Frame: Centuries of Racial Framing and Counter-Framing* (New York: Routledge, 2010); Adia H. Wingfield and Joe Feagin, "The Racial Dialectic: President Barack Obama and the White Racial Frame," *Qualitative Sociology* 35, no. 2 (2012): 144.

20. Charis E. Kubrin, Marjorie S. Zazt, and Ramiro Martinez, eds, *Punishing Immigrants: Policy, Politics, and Injustice* (New York: New York University Press, 2012); Rubén G. Rumbaut and Walter A. Ewing, *The Myth of Immigrant Criminality and the Paradox of Assimilation* (Washington, DC: American Immigration Law Foundation, 2007), http://www.immigrationpolicy.org.

21. J. Blascovich, W. B. Mendes, S. B. Hunter, B. Lickel, and N. Kowai-Bell, "Perceived Threat in Social Interactions with Stigmatized Others," *Journal of Personality and Social Psychology* 80 (February 2001): 253–67; Hazel Rose Markus and Alana Conner, *Clash! 8 Cultural Conflicts That Make Us Who We Are* (New York: Hudson Street Books, 2013).

22. Amandla Stenberg, "Don't Cash Crop My Cornrows: A Crash Discourse on Black Culture," April 15, 2015, https://www.youtube.com.

23. Chandra L. Jackson, Frank B. Hu, Susan Redline, David R. Williams, Josiemer Mattei, and Ichiro Kawachi, "Racial/Ethnic Disparities in Short Sleep Duration by Occupation: The Contribution of Immigrant Status," *Social Science & Medicine* 118 (October 2014): 71–79.

24. Robert J. Sampson and Alix S. Winter, "The Racial Ecology of Lead Poisoning: Toxic Inequality in Chicago Neighborhoods, 1995–2013," *Du Bois Review: Social Science Research on Race* 13 (Winter 2016): 279.

25. Stenberg, "Don't Cash Crop My Cornrows."

CHAPTER 3: WHO, ME? I'M NOT A RACIST, BUT . . .

1. Eduardo Bonilla-Silva, *Racism without Racists: Color-Blind Racism and the Persistence of Racial Inequality in the United States* (Lanham, MD: Rowman & Littlefield, 2003), 4.

2. James M. Jones, John F. Dovidio, and Deborah L. Vietze, *The Psychology of Diversity: Beyond Prejudice and Racism* (Malden, MA: Wiley Blackwell, 2014).

3. Claude M. Steele, *Whistling Vivaldi and Other Clues to How Stereotypes Affect Us* (New York: W. W. Norton, 2010).

4. Jennifer L. Eberhardt, *Biased: Uncovering the Hidden Prejudice That Shapes What We See, Think, and Do* (New York: Viking, 2019).

5. Gary Orfield and Erica Frankenberg, *Brown at 60: Great Progress, A Long Retreat, and an Uncertain Future*, Civil Rights Project/Proyecto Derechos Civiles, University of California–Los Angeles, 2014; Gary Orfield, *Schools More Separate: Consequences of a Decade of Resegregation* (Cambridge, MA: Civil Rights Project, Harvard University, 2001); Lawrence D. Bobo, "Inequalities That Endure? Racial Ideology, American Politics, and the Peculiar Role of the Social Sciences," in *The Changing Terrain of Race and Ethnicity*, ed. Maria Krysan and Amanda E. Lewis (New York: Russell Sage Foundation, 2004), 13–42.

6. Juliana Menasce Horowitz, Anna Brown, and Kiana Cox, *Most Americans Say Trump's Election Has Led to Worse Race Relations in the U.S.* (Washington, DC: Pew Research Center, 2019), accessed May 15, 2019, https://www.pew socialtrends.org/2019/04/09/how-americans-see-the-state-of-race-relations; Anna Brown, *Key Findings on Americans' Views of Race in 2019* (Washington, DC: Pew Research Center, 2019), accessed May 15, 2019, https://www.pew research.org/fact-tank/2019/04/09key-findings-on-americans-views-of-race -in-2019.

7. Rachel Wetts and Robb Willer, "Privilege on the Precipice: Perceived Racial Status Threats Led White Americans to Oppose Welfare Programs," *Social Forces* 97 (December 2018): 793–822.

8. Steven Miller, "Economic Anxiety or Racial Resentment? An Evaluation of Attitudes Toward Immigration in the U.S. from 1992 to 2016." Working Paper, Clemson University, 2019.

9. Bonilla-Silva, *Racism without Racists*.

10. Stokely Carmichael and Charles V. Hamilton, *Black Power: The Politics of Liberation* (New York: Vintage, 1967).

11. Joe R. Feagin, *Racist America: Current Realities and Future Reparations*, 3rd ed. (New York: Routledge, 2014).

12. Peggy McIntosh, "White Privilege and Male Privilege: A Personal Account of Coming to See Correspondences through Work in Women's Studies," Working Paper 189, Wellesley Centers for Women, 1983.

13. Kristina R. Olson, Carol S. Dweck, Elizabeth S. Spelke, and Mahzarin Banaji, "Children's Reponses to Group-Based Inequalities: Perpetuation and Rectification," *Social Cognition* 29, no. 2 (2011): 270–87.

14. Robin Diangelo, *White Fragility: Why It's So Hard for White People to Talk about Racism* (Boston: Beacon, 2018).

15. Mitch Berbrier, "The Victim Ideology of White Supremacists and White Separatists in the United States," *Sociological Focus* 32 (May 2000): 175–91.

16. Bonilla-Silva, *Racism without Racists*.

17. Bobo, "Inequalities That Endure?"

CHAPTER 4: WHAT DID YOU SAY? CONTESTING COMMON-SENSE RACISM

1. Susan Haas, "Taylor Swift Makes Rare Political Statement, Backing Democrat in Tennessee Senate Race," *USA TODAY*, October 7, 2018, https://www.usatoday.com/story/life/2018/10/07/taylor-swift-getting-gasp-political-instagram-post/1562123002.

2. Kayla Fontenot, Jessica Semega, and Melissa Kollar, *Income and Poverty in the United States: 2017* (Washington, DC: US Census Bureau, 2018); Gary Orfield, Erica Frankenberg, and Laurie Russman, *School Resegregation and Civil Rights Challenges for the Obama Administration*, Civil Rights Project/Proyecto Derechos Civiles, University of California–Los Angeles, 2014, https://www.civilrightsproject.ucla.edu; E. Ann Carson, *Prisoners in 2016* (Washington, DC: Bureau of Justice Statistics, US Department of Justice, National Center for Health Statistics, 2018); *Health United States 2018* (Hyattsville, MD: National Center for Health Statistics, 2018), https://cdc.gov.

3. Joe R. Feagin, *The White Racial Frame: Centuries of Racial Framing and Counter-Framing* (New York: Routledge, 2010).

4. Paul Ryan, radio interview, *Morning in America*, March 12, 2014.

5. Center on Budget and Policy Priorities, *Chart Book: SNAP Helps Struggling Families Put Food on the Table* (Washington, DC: Center on Budget and Policy Priorities, 2018), https://www.cbpp.org.

6. See https://www.cbpp.org/research/food-assistance/a-quick-guide-to-snap-eligibility-and-benefits.

7. Susan D. Greenbaum, *Blaming the Poor: The Long Shadow of the Moynihan Report on Cruel Images about Poverty* (New Brunswick, NJ: Rutgers University Press, 2015).

8. Kathryn Edin and Maria Kefalas, *Promises I Can Keep: Why Poor Women Put Marriage before Motherhood* (Berkeley: University of California Press, 2005).

9. Lydia Saad, *Fewer See Equal Opportunity for Blacks in Jobs, Housing* (Princeton, NJ: Gallup Organization, 2019), https://news.gallup.com/opinion/gallup/246137/fewer-equal-opportunity-blacks-jobs-housing.aspx.

10. William Julius Wilson, *The Truly Disadvantaged: The Inner City, the Underclass, and Public Policy* (Chicago: University of Chicago Press, 1987); William Julius Wilson, *The Declining Significance of Race: Blacks and Changing American Institutions* (Chicago: University of Chicago Press, 1978); William Julius Wilson, *When Work Disappears: The World of the New Urban Poor* (Chicago: University of Chicago Press, 1997).

11. Margaret L. Andersen and Patricia Hill Collins, *Race, Class, and Gender: Intersections and Inequalities*, 10th ed. (Boston: Cengage, 2020).

12. Gloria T. Hull (Akasha), Patricia Bell Scott, and Barbara Smith, *All the Women Are White, All the Blacks Are Men, But Some of Us Are Brave* (New York: Feminist Press, 2015).

13. Ana Gonzalez-Barrera and Jens Manuel Krogstad, *What We Know about Illegal Immigration from Mexico* (Washington, DC: Pew Research Center, 2018),

accessed May 21, 2019, https://www.pewresearch.org/fact-tank/2018/12/03
/what-we-know-about-illegal-immigration-from-mexico.
14. National Immigration Forum, *Fact Sheet: Immigrants and Public Benefits*
(Washington, DC: National Immigration Forum, 2018), accessed May 21,
2019, https://immigrationforum.org/article/fact-sheet-immigrants-and
-public-benefits; Purvi Sevak and Lucie Schmidt, "Immigrants and Retire-
ment Resources," *Social Security Bulletin* 74, no. 1 (2014): 27–45.
15. Rebecca Riffkin, *Higher Support for Gender Affirmative Action Than Race*
(Princeton, NJ: Gallup Organization, 2015), accessed May 21, 2019, https://
news.gallup.com/poll/184772/higher-support-gender-affirmative
-action-race.aspx; Frank Newport, *The Harvard Affirmative Action Case and
Public Opinion* (Princeton, NJ: Gallup Organization, 2018), https://news
.gallup.com/opinion/polling-matters/243965/harvard-affirmative-action-case
-public-opinion.aspx.
16. Patricia Gurin, E. L. Dey, and Sylvia Hurtado, "Diversity and Higher Education: Theory and Impact on Educational Outcomes," *Harvard Educational
Review* 72, no. 3 (2002): 330–66.

CHAPTER 5: BUT THAT WAS THEN—I DIDN'T HAVE ANYTHING TO DO WITH IT

1. James Baldwin, "The White Problem in America," *Ebony*, August 1965;
reprinted in James Baldwin, *The Price of the Ticket: Collected Nonfiction, 1948–
1985* (New York: St. Martin's, 1985), 410.
2. Gustavo López, Neil G. Luiz, and Eileen Patten, *Key Facts about Asian Americans, a Diverse and Growing Population* (Washington, DC: Pew Research Center, 2017), accessed May 20, 2019, https://www.pewresearch.org/fact-tank/2017
/09/08/key-facts-about-asian-americans.
3. Chuck Collins, Dedrick Asana-Muhammed, Josh Hoxie, and Sabrina Terry,
Dreams Deferred: How Enriching the 1% Widens the Racial Wealth Divide (Washington, DC: Institute for Policy Studies, 2019), accessed May 20, 2019, https://
ips-dc.org/racial-wealth-divide-2019; Darrick Hamilton and Trevon Logan,
"Here's Why Black Families Have Struggled for Decades to Gain Wealth,"
MarketWatch, 2019, accessed May 21, 2019, https://www.marketwatch
.com/story/heres-why-black-families-have-struggled-for-decades-to-gain
-wealth-2019-02-28; Melvin Oliver and Thomas M. Shapiro, "Disrupting
the Racial Wealth Gap," *Contexts* 18 (Winter 2019): 17–21.
4. Melvin Oliver and Thomas M. Shapiro, *Black Wealth/White Wealth: A New
Perspective on Racial Inequality*, 2nd ed. (New York: Routledge, 2006).
5. Bruce Mitchell and Juan Franco, *HOLC "Redlining" Maps: The Persistent
Structure of Segregation and Economic Inequality* (Washington, DC: National
Community Reinvestment Coalition, 2018), accessed May 21, 2019, https://
ncrc.org/wp-content/uploads/dlm_uploads/2018/02/NCRC-Research-HOLC
-10.pdf.

6. Richard Rothstein, *The Color of Law: A Forgotten History of How Our Government Segregated America* (New York: Liveright, 2017).

7. Ira Katznelson, *When Affirmative Action Was White: An Untold History of Racial Inequality in Twentieth-Century America* (New York: W. W. Norton, 2005); Rothstein, *Color of Law*.

8. Rothstein, *Color of Law*, 85.

9. Rothstein, *Color of Law*, 182.

10. Katznelson, *When Affirmative Action Was White*.

11. Lyndon Johnson, Commencement Address, Howard University, 1965.

12. Peter Kolchin, *American Slavery, 1619–1877* (New York: Hill and Wang, 1993), 29.

13. Ron Takaki, *Strangers from a Different Shore: A History of Asian Americans* (Boston: Little, Brown, 1989); Ronald Takaki, *A Different Mirror: A History of Multicultural America* (Boston: Little, Brown, 1993).

14. Carole Marks, *Farewell—We're Good and Gone* (Bloomington: Indiana University Press, 1989); Diana Edkins and Carole Marks, *The Power of Pride: Stylebreakers and Rulemakers of the Harlem Renaissance* (New York: Crown, 1989); Isabel Wilkerson, *The Warmth of Other Suns: The Epic Story of America's Great Migration* (New York: Vintage, 2011).

15. Albert Camarillo, *Chicanos in a Changing Society* (Dallas: Southern Methodist University Press, 1979), 18, 182.

16. Nicholas De Genova and Ana Y. Ramos-Zayab, *Latino Crossings: Mexicans, Puerto Ricans, and the Politics of Race and Citizenship* (New York: Routledge, 2003); Rodolfo F. Acuña, *Occupied America: A History of Chicanos*, 8th ed. (Upper Saddle River, NJ: Pearson, 2014); Gilbert Paul Carrasco, "Latinos in the United States: Invitation and Exile," in *The Latino Condition*, 2nd ed., ed. Richard Delgado and Jean Stefanic (New York: New York University Press, 2010), 78–85.

17. Camarillo, *Chicanos in a Changing Society*, 18, 182.

18. Takaki, *A Different Mirror*; Joe R. Feagin and José A. Cobas, *Latinos Facing Racism: Discrimination, Resistance, and Endurance* (Boulder, CO: Paradigm, 2014).

19. Douglas S. Massey, "Foreword," in *Latinas/os in the United States: Changing the Face of America*, ed. Havidán Rodríquez, Rogelio Sáenz, and Cecilia Menjívar (New York: Springer, 2008), xi–xiii.

20. Michael A. Olivas, "My Grandfather's Stories and Immigration Law," in *The Latino Condition*, 2nd ed., ed. Richard Delgado and Jean Stefanic (New York: New York University Press, 2010), 223–28; Ricardo Romo, "Mexican Americans: Their Civic and Political Incorporation," in *Origins and Destinies: Immigration, Race, and Ethnicity in America*, ed. Silvia Pedraza and Rubén G. Rumbaut (Belmont, CA: Wadsworth, 1996), 84–97.

21. Takaki, *A Different Mirror*.

22. Esther Ngan-Ling Chow, "Family, Economy, and the State: A Legacy of Struggle for Chinese American Women," in *Origins and Destinies: Immigration,*

Race, and Ethnicity in America, ed. Silvia Pedraza and Rubén G. Rumbaut (Belmont, CA: Wadsworth, 1996), 110–24; Takaki, *A Different Mirror*.
23. Takaki, *A Different Mirror*.
24. Gordon H. Chang, *Ghosts of Gold Mountain: The Epic Story of the Chinese Who Built the Transcontinental Railroad* (Boston: Houghton Mifflin Harcourt, 2019).
25. Bonnie Thornton Dill, "Our Mothers' Grief: Racial-Ethnic Women and the Maintenance of Families," *Journal of Family History* 13 (October 1988): 415–83; Takaki, *Strangers from a Different Shore*.
26. Evelyn Nakano Glenn and Rhacel Salazar Parrañes, "The Other Issei: Japanese Immigrant Women in the Pre–World War II Period," in *Origins and Destinies: Immigration, Race, and Ethnicity in America*, ed. Silvia Pedraza and Rubén G. Rumbaut (Belmont, CA: Wadsworth, 1996), 125–40; Evelyn Nakano Glenn, *Issei, Nisei, War Bride: Three Generations of Japanese American Women in Domestic Service* (Philadelphia: Temple University Press, 1986).
27. Takaki, *A Different Mirror*.
28. Camarillo, *Chicanos in a Changing Society*; Olivas, "My Grandfather's Stories"; Carrasco, "Latinos in the United States"; Havidán Rodríquez, Rogelio Sáenz, and Cecilia Menjívar, eds. *Latinas/os in the United States: Changing the Face of America* (New York: Springer, 2008).
29. Neil Foley, "Over the Rainbow: *Hernandez v. Texas, Brown v. Board of Education*, and *Black v. Brown*," *UCLA Chicano-Latina Law Review* 25 (Spring 2005): 139–52; Maria Blanco, "Before *Brown*, There was *Mendez*: The Lasting Impact of *Mendez v. Westminster* in the Struggle for Desegregation," *Perspectives* (March 2010), http://www.immigrationpolicy.org.
30. Anna Brown and Eileen Patten, *Hispanics of Puerto Rican Origin in the United States, 2011* (Washington, DC: US Census Bureau, 2011), https://www.census.gov; Héctor A. Carrasquillo and Virginia Sánchez-Korrol, "Migration, Community, and Culture: The United States–Puerto Rican Experience," in *Origins and Destinies: Immigration, Race, and Ethnicity in America*, ed. Silvia Pedraza and Rubén G. Rumbaut (Belmont, CA: Wadsworth, 1996), 98–109.
31. Michelle Obama, *Becoming* (New York: Crown, 2018), 7.
32. William Faulkner, *Requiem for a Nun* (New York: Random House, 1951), 73.
33. Jon Stewart, *The Daily Show*, June 19, 2015.
34. Maya Angelou, "On the Pulse of Morning," poem read at the inauguration of President William Clinton, Washington, DC, January 20, 1993.

Chapter 6: Getting Smart about Race, Then Doing Something about It

1. Sonia Sotomayor, *My Beloved World* (New York: Knopf), 164.
2. Cherrie Moraga and Gloria E. Anzaldua, eds., *This Bridge Called My Back: Writings by Radical Women of Color* (New York: Kitchen Table Press, 1981).

3. Martin Luther King Jr., "I Have a Dream" (speech, Lincoln Memorial, Washington, DC, August 28, 1963).

4. Patricia Gurin, E. L. Dey, and Sylvia Hurtado, "Diversity and Higher Education: Theory and Impact on Educational Outcomes," *Harvard Educational Review* 72, no. 3 (2002): 330–66.

5. Frank Newport, *The Harvard Affirmative Action Case and Public Opinion* (Princeton, NJ: Gallup Organization, 2018), accessed May 15, 2019, https://news.gallup.com/opinion/polling-matters/243965/harvard-affirmative-action-case-public-opinion.aspx.

6. *Regents of University of California v. Bakke*, 438 U.S. 625 (1978).

7. W. E. B. Du Bois, *The Souls of Black Folk* (New York: Penguin, 1996 [1903]).

8. Kim Parker, Nikki Graf, and Ruth Igielnik, *Generation Z Looks a Lot Like Millennials on Key Social and Political Issues* (Washington, DC: Pew Research Center, 2019), accessed May 15, 2019, https://www.pewsocialtrends.org/2019/01/17/generation-z-looks-a-lot-like-millennials-on-key-social-and-political-issues.

9. Lewis M. Killian, *The Impossible Revolution? Black Power and the American Dream* (New York: Random House, 1968).

Index

Page numbers for figures are italicized.

Black History Month, 119
Black men: health, 42; middle
  class, 80, 84, 137–138;
  prison, 70; segregation
  among, 30; wealth,
  98–101
Blackmun, Harry, 133
Black women: as intellectuals,
  83; as domestic workers,
  109; stereotypes of, 40
blaming the victim,
  74–79, 124
Blumenbach, Johann, 8
Bonilla-Silva, Eduardo, 18,
  47, 65
Boston, xvi
Bowers, Robert Gregory,
  92–93
bracero program, 116
Brebrier, Mitch, 64
Brokaw, Tom, 85
Brown v. Board of Education,
  xvi, 31, 116–117

Cambodians, 17
Carmen, Miranda, 37
Carmichael, Stokely, 59
Catholics, 50; stereotypes
  of, 39
Caucasian, xx; origins of, 7–8,
  13–14
census, US, 10–12
Charlottesville, VA, 49, 92

chattel, defined, 107
Chinese Americans, 17–18;
  history of, 112–114;
  as miners, 80–81;
  as railroad workers,
  112–113; stereotypes of,
  39; as strikebreakers, 81;
  women, 112
Chinese Exclusion Act of
  1882, 113–114
Chiquita Banana, 36–37
Civil Rights Movement, 30,
  51, 80, 88, 135
Civil War, 8, 13
class. *See* social class
class conflict, 80–81, 90–92
color-blind racism, 65–68,
  130–132
The Color of Fear, 72–73
commonsense racism, 69–94,
  124; defined, 71
concentrated poverty, 33
controlling images, 37–41
criminalization, 38–39
criminal justice, 70
Crusius, Patrick Wood, xi, 25,
  39, 134
Cuban Americans, 18, 86
cultural racism, 35–41
cultural values, 71; as
  explanation of racial
  inequality, 71, 74–79
culture of affirmation, 44–45

About the Author

Margaret L. Andersen (PhD, MA, University of Massachusetts, Amherst; BA, Georgia State University) is the Edward F. and Elizabeth Goodman Rosenberg Professor Emerita at the University of Delaware. She is the author of several books, including *Race in Society: The Enduring American Dilemma*; *Thinking about Women*, now in its eleventh edition; the best-selling anthology *Race, Class, and Gender*, 10th ed. (coedited with Patricia Hill Collins); *Race and Ethnicity in Society: The Changing Landscape*, 4th ed. (coedited with Elizabeth Higginbotham); *Sociology: The Essentials*, 10th ed. (coauthored with Howard F. Taylor); *Living Art: The Life of African American Art Collector Paul Jones*; and *On Land and on Sea: A Century of Women in the Rosenfeld Collection*.

She is an emeritus member of the National Advisory Board for Stanford University's Center for Comparative Studies in Race and Ethnicity, Past Vice President of the American Sociological Association, and Past President of the Eastern Sociological Society. She currently coaches faculty in the Faculty Success Program of the National Center for Faculty Development and Diversity. She has served in several senior administrative positions at the University of Delaware, including Vice Provost for Faculty Affairs and Diversity, Executive Director of the President's Diversity Initiative, Interim Deputy Provost, and Dean of the College of Arts and Sciences, among others.

Andersen has received two teaching awards from the University of Delaware and two prestigious awards from her professional organizations: the Eastern Sociological Society Merit Award for career contributions and the American Sociological Association's Jessie Bernard Award, given for expanding the boundaries of sociology to include women. In recognition of her scholarship, teaching, and service, in 2017 the University of Delaware granted her an honorary Doctor of Laws degree.